Unworthy

Unworthy

How to Stop Hating Yourself

ANNELI RUFUS

JEREMY P. TARCHER/PENGUIN
a member of Penguin Group (USA)
New York

JEREMY P. TARCHER/PENGUIN
Published by the Penguin Group
Penguin Group (USA) LLC
375 Hudson Street
New York, New York 10014

USA · Canada · UK · Ireland · Australia
New Zealand · India · South Africa · China

penguin.com
A Penguin Random House Company

First trade paperback edition 2015
Copyright © 2014 by Anneli Rufus

Most Tarcher/Penguin books are available at special quantity discounts for bulk purchase for sales promotions, premiums, fund-raising, and educational needs. Special books or book excerpts also can be created to fit specific needs. For details, write: Special.Markets@us.penguingroup.com.

The Library of Congress has cataloged the hardcover edition as follows:

Rufus, Anneli S.
Unworthy : how to stop hating yourself / Anneli Rufus.
p.   cm.
Includes bibliographical references.
ISBN 978-0-399-16421-7
1. Self-esteem.   I. Title.
BF697.5.S46R876   2014   2013050137
158.1—dc23

ISBN 978-0-399-17513-8 (trade paperback)

Printed in the United States of America
3   5   7   9   10   8   6   4

Book design by Gretchen Achilles

This book is for:

MGR

KNL

Contents

Unworthy

Introduction

The most terrible and violent of our own afflictions
is to despise our own beings.
—MICHEL DE MONTAIGNE

For more than forty years, I hated myself unreservedly, as if
it was required. Why? Was I a murderer? A thief? Had I
committed genocide or bombed the Prado? Was I mean? Did I
have seven swollen, scaly heads? Whose children had I thrown
down wells? Which city did I plunder? Had I put soap in a
swimming pool or slaughtered fawns?

No. None of those. I hated myself because Mom hated herself and, meaning no harm, taught me how. Self-loathing
spreads that way, from heart to heart and hand to hand. For
decades, I avoided mirrors, called myself the worst words you
can think of, skipped meals, and stared jealously at strangers,
wishing I was anyone but me. Spectacles of my eighteen thousand days of hate.

I've seen what self-loathing can do. I've seen it steal the light
right out of eyes. I've watched it drive the beautiful, the brilliant,
and the kind to places from which they could not come back.

What if, instead of what actually happened on those days, I

had drawn eighteen thousand portraits or learned eighteen thousand Estonian words? I would be fluent now! I would have a portfolio!

What would you do today if you did not despise yourself?

. . .

Science tells us that no one is born with low self-esteem. Recent research suggests that some people are genetically more susceptible to develop low self-esteem at some point in life, just as some people are born more likely than most to sing well or go bald. But in this crowded, complex world, self-loathing can seize anyone at any moment. No one is immune.

Five people I have known:

On her first-ever ski trip, Cara teetered at the top of the bunny slope, took one tentative step, then fell face-first into the powder. Twice she struggled back to her feet, only to fall. Her fiancé and their friends offered encouragement, but Cara unlaced her ski boots, ran back to the lodge sobbing, and stayed in her room for the rest of the trip.

Accepting his third annual Teacher of the Year award, Jeremy gazed out at an auditorium packed with wildly applauding children, parents, and colleagues. Silently he mourned: *I was supposed to get my doctorate. I should be famous by now, not teaching fourth grade. I was supposed to have made earthshaking discoveries. It was expected of me. And I failed.*

Rachel held in her stomach as Mister Married Guy slid his hand under her blouse. *Sexy eyes*, murmured Mister Married Guy. Rachel laughed. *My best feature. My only feature, compensating for this fat gut and these giant thighs.* Mister Married Guy was not listening. Hours later, home again, Rachel hurled books at the wall while screaming, *I wanna diiiiie.*

The boss rebuked Nate for his new designs: *Clearly you lack the skills claimed on your résumé.* Nate flinched, remembering what the neighborhood bullies used to say as they spat into his lunch. *You're right,* Nate said. *I suck.* His coworkers gasped as Nate snatched his designs from the boss and tore them up, growling, *I suck! Screw you! Screw everything!*

Handing the clerk her credit card, Alison hoped her new friend Skye would like the gift. Just as she hoped her sister had liked the Hermès scarf that Alison had sent her from Paris. And just as she hoped her son liked his new Air Jordans and private tennis lessons. Watching the clerk wrap Skye's gift, a two-hundred-dollar designer handbag, Alison hoped it was enough.

Gifts to please others.

"I've always had really low self-esteem," Mariah Carey said in an interview after having released eleven CDs, acted in five Hollywood films, and won more than two hundred music awards. "And I still do."

The weird thing about self-esteem is how little connection it bears to reality. Many burglars and murderers feel great about themselves. Yet many upstanding citizens whom a jury of sages would declare kind, wonderful, and worthy hate themselves.

A silent epidemic grips the land. The afflicted include many whom you would least suspect, even the ones you think have everything, even some of the bravest and (in your eyes, but not theirs) the best.

The hoary stereotypes of the person with low self-esteem as a timorous Woody Allen character, beaten wife, serial killer, or

fearful, suffering

3

Dickensian waif are exactly that: hoary stereotypes. The real picture includes Cara, Jeremy, Rachel, Nate, Alison, Mariah, you, me, and who knows how many more of us, of every stripe. What are we doing here together, side by side? We share something. Not something you would notice right away. Not something we discuss or something you could touch. We dislike ourselves for no valid reason. Monitoring ourselves and regretting nearly every act, some of us even loathe ourselves. Despise ourselves. Call ourselves names you would not call a dog. We do this, or we did. We are six among multitudes.

In this book I say *we who hate ourselves* in the present tense, although for me it is no longer eminently true, at least not all the time, at least not as it was. But *we who hate ourselves* was for so many years the only legion I had ever known. Its refrains remain in my mind forever fresh. If marching with my former legion can lead it to freedom, march with it I will.

We who hate ourselves think we have huge flaws—ugliness, say, or sloppiness. We think these flaws legitimize our self-loathing. We focus on them with obsessive tunnel vision, which obscures our other, better qualities. We do not realize that our flaws—and who is flawless?—are not our big problem. Low self-esteem is.

Imagine having little or no self-esteem when everyone expects you to have lots. Self-esteem is an industry these days, a given, the major religion of this era—yet we have little or none. Not in a good way, not as in some kind of ego-shedding Buddhist selflessness. It's not as if we who hate ourselves have *transcended* self-esteem.

I do not say all this in search of sympathy. I would rather not

[handwritten margin note:] Or lack of : -intelligence -Purity. -attributes to go to heaven

speak of self-esteem at all—mine, yours, or anyone's. I would rather not have to. I would rather be invisible to you and/or discussing pearl-diving instead, or clairvoyance, or Thebes. But as long as this epidemic rages, driving the afflicted to curse, cut, and kill themselves, we need to talk.

You have climbed this far. Despite everything, you have. You were the Child with Far to Go and you have come, helping others along the way. If you picked up a magic pebble on the beach and found that it could speak, that it possessed the power to describe you accurately, that its mission was to tell you what is good about you, okay about you, and not so good, and that it could not lie, what would it say?

To casual observers, I look like a middle-size American with a middle-size, ordinary life. Casual observers do not know how many years I wasted on self-loathing, that school and work and relationships flashed past almost unseen as I faced forward, blind with fear, and backward, burning with regret. Casual observers do not know that self-loathing was really my career.

We lost our self-esteem in sandboxes and swimming pools and sleazy bars. We lost it in attics and open fields. However you lost yours, most of us who hate ourselves display the same "tells"—the same habits, reactions, defenses, and coping skills: dead giveaways by which we can identify each other and which we can change—as we will see later in this book.

Unlike others who are united in their suffering, we who hate ourselves tend to suffer in insular silence because we believe so ardently that we are bad and thus (a) no one wants to be around us, much less hear us mope, and (b) our badness gives us no choice but to hate ourselves. So what's to say?

We who hate ourselves think we do not deserve solidarity.

Because self-loathing is the curse that dares not speak its name.

Q. *How does someone with low self-esteem screw in a lightbulb?*

A. *However you want me to! Is this way okay? Is it? Really? No. It's not. Totally not. Oh man. I can't believe I screwed it in wrong, like I screw all lightbulbs in wrong. I screw everything in wrong.*

Why should you slog through a whole book about self-loathing? A whole book about feeling miserable, anxious, and cursed? You shouldn't. And that's not this book. It might appear that way at first, but no: we are not here to whine (okay, maybe just a bit) but to work.

This book is about setting down the weapons we use on ourselves—just for a minute at a time and *shhh*, no one need see—and pondering the possibility that they are not required, not justified, not right—and never were. That they were thrust into our arms by others long ago. That we are wielding them by accident, through deceit, by mistake. What if you heard a jingling sound at work one day and glanced under your desk to notice a ball and chain clamped to your ankle? *How long has that been there?* you'd ask yourself. *So that's why it's been taking me so long to climb upstairs.*

So ponder, even merely theoretically at first, the notion that you hate yourself by happenstance and not because you

should. That your self-loathing is a concept, a philosophy, a leg-
acy, an entity that you adopted somewhere back there just as
people adopt new philosophies when joining cults. That your
self-loathing is someone else's philosophy: an individual's, society's, a clique's—thrust upon you when you were young and/or
trusting and/or aiming to please.

And ponder, even lightly, just as opening a window sends
air rustling through a room, the notion that whatever stole your
self-esteem was not actually about you. That none of this was
ever about you. You only thought it was.

Suspending all other beliefs for a split second, consider the
idea that you were tricked. The good news is that now the trick
has been revealed as such. Once that happens—say, in a card
trick or a magic trick—a trick no longer works.

Was it prejudice that played this trick on you? Or was it expectations of accomplishment, obedience, inclusion, loyalty, or
conformity? Subtle, unspoken cruelty or outright abuse? Was it
a million tiny things you never even noticed happening, nothing direct or obvious but gestures, glances, images on billboards,
yearnings disallowed that left you comparing yourself to everyone and, in your own eyes, falling short? Or was it love? Well-
meant guidance gone wrong? Catastrophe? Words overheard?
Who put those weapons into your hands, and where are those
perpetrators now? What are they doing as we speak? Are they
thinking of you? Can they even recall your name or face?

Do they deserve what you have given them? Did they merit
your sacrifice?

This is a book about healing and hope. I just need you to

know that. It includes strategies and tactics and lessons to lead us out of here. But first we need to understand how we fell into this predicament and how it looks and feels and sounds. We need to realize where we are before we can move on.

This path starts in the dark.

. . .

Admittedly, it's hard to start, because we tell ourselves: If you try, you will fail. If you stand, you will fall. Would you say such words to a friend, a child, even a stranger? No? Eureka! You've already started. You're up on your feet.

Hidden within what feels like the crippling inertia of self-loathing is a secret fuel. What is self-loathing but negative energy? Horrible, sure, but energy. And fierce. What if we simply saw this energy as energy? We weren't just sitting there! We spent years regretting our every act and talking ourselves out of everything! What if in witnessing this raw power and creativity we saw ourselves as capable of strength? What if with new awareness we could harness this strength, redirect it, channel it, transform its substance into something else, focused perhaps *outside* us—on adventure, say, or empathy, or boundless curiosity?

Feeling your worst is not that different from feeling your strongest.

. . .

I told someone with high self-esteem that I was writing a book about low self-esteem. *Low self-esteem,* she parried, *is a choice.*

Technically, yes. Totally, no. *Getting* low self-esteem is *not* a choice. We did not choose whatever trauma took us here.

Continuing to hate ourselves? This is the tricky part. *This* is a choice that does not feel like one.

Yes, hating oneself and then no longer hating oneself is a voluntary shift. But because we believe our self-loathing is justified, we believe ourselves no more capable of quelling it than of changing our DNA.

Because we are convinced that we *deserve* to hate ourselves, vowing to stop sounds radical, rebellious, and ridiculous. Self-loathing is, to us, an obligation, a necessity. Unlike most other emotional problems, self-loathing includes a diabolical self-destruct mechanism that confounds most attempts to disarm it. Integral to self-loathing is the delusion that the condition is not just inescapable but *deserved*, such that trying to extricate oneself from its clutches feels like a betrayal of life's natural order. The ostensible rectitude of our self-loathing feels confirmed and reconfirmed with every breakup, every job we don't get, every rude comment from cabdrivers and passersby. So even if we *could* see a pathway to happiness and self-acceptance, we would hesitate to take it. Our recovery seems an affront to cosmic justice.

Fine. Let's affront justice.

We have spent too long believing lies about ourselves that we had no idea were lies but that instead became our codes of ethics, weltanschauungs, liturgies, and lexicons. We believed we were ugly, stupid, inadequate, lazy, and unlovable, even evil. We believed this because somewhere back there we were told it was true—told this once or often, vaguely or verbatim.

Directly or indirectly, intentionally or by accident, once or over and over, we were philosophically abused.

Once we started hating ourselves, we did not understand why everything hurt or that it need not. If we pondered this hurt as such, we believed that it occurred because we deserved it.

We the afflicted, we who hate ourselves, need to know that thinking, acting, and feeling came so easily to those with self-respect; that these seemingly simple processes—thinking, acting, and feeling, thus including hope and love—are monumentally difficult for us, requiring twice as much effort on our part as others have to expend. For us, even a simple task—dressing, ordering food in restaurants—means thinking, over-thinking, unthinking, striding through thick waves of shame, dread, and fear. That sounds ludicrously like an act of courage.

And the casual observer does not know and should not know—because whoever does not know is blessed.

* * *

Have you ever viewed a group photograph that included you and felt a wave of nausea, a lurch that hit you with a jolt of recognition when you thought: *I knew I looked bad but not THAT bad?*

I have. I thought: *Could that listless-haired, torn-jeansed, slouching castaway among those shining angel-girls really be me?*

Well, yeah. If you were making an entirely appearance-based comparison, it could.

The other women in the photograph are young enough to be my children. They are athletes. I am not. They dress well. I do not. My legs are different lengths, which makes me slouch. Their legs all match. Judged strictly by appearance, those women and I are factually, chronologically, and orthopedically in different leagues.

But we who hate ourselves compare ourselves nonstop in not just one dimension but all dimensions to others—all others—and always in our estimations come up short. *I'm less serene than that guy.* Yes, but he's a Buddhist monk. *That woman is way sexier than I am.* Sure, but she's a Victoria's Secret model. *These sunglasses look better on my teenage son than on me.* Yes. He's a teenage son. Would you race a walrus against a bee? Why not? And aren't you just as good or better at *some* things than are the monk, the model, and your son? And honestly, who cares? And wouldn't it be sweet relief to simply set aside the scorecard and the calipers and stroll away?

* * *

Here is life with low self-esteem:

I never dream of home.

I always dream of unfamiliar landscapes: shores and skyscrapers but never anywhere I even recognize, much less have lived or loved. In dreams I am forever lost.

But also this:

For years and years, something strange happened every few days as I woke.

I saw a fist.

Saw it with my closed eyes, inside my mind. It wore a scuffed

11

white boxing glove. Fast as a flash, it surged out of the darkness on the right side of my head and punched me in the face.

Sometimes it struck my cheekbone or my teeth, often my eye. Not once. Not twice. Rapid-fire, *bam-bam-bam-bam*, as in boxing rings, but so relentless, so efficiently precise, that sometimes semiconsciously I mused that the fist was not human but affixed to a steel rod extending from some sinister machine.

In real life, one such punch could shatter bone, draw blood, or send vitreous humor streaking through the air. In real life, such a punch would make you duck, dodge, put up some defense, or die. Yet nearly every dawn for nearly all my life I lay unmoving as the punches came. Lids closed, I watched the white glove almost calmly, an imaginary recoil racing down my spine. Then I opened my eyes. Another day. But with a secret message: *bam-bam-bam!*

Self-loathing manifests in many ways. Some of these ways are obvious: the tears, the cuts, the guns. But most the public never sees.

The secret self-recriminations: I'm ugly. I failed. I'm inadequate, insufficient, boring, not as cool or complete or smart or successful as that person over there or her or him or them. Comparisons: me vs. everyone. That grueling, grinding *drip-drip-drip*. Don't look at me. Why won't you look at me? What's wrong with me? The raw rip of regret.

> *A person with low self-esteem walks into a bar.*
> *"What'll you have?" the bartender asks.*
> *"I don't know!" screams the person with low self-esteem. "I don't fucking know!"*

Self-esteem spans a spectrum. At one end is all-out, worship-me, dictator-style narcissism. At the other end is abject self-loathing, which in truth is narcissism too—negative narcissism: mirror, mirror, upside down.

Those standing safely at the midpoint of the self-esteem spectrum feel okay about themselves. Not great, not horrible, just okay. They don't expect straight As every semester, especially if they haven't studied much. They don't expect to become CEOs their first week at work or to always win.

Nor do they expect straight Fs, to be fired their first week at work, or always lose. Aware that they are better at some things than at others, those in the middle of the self-esteem spectrum assess themselves accurately, celebrating their strengths and tolerating their weaknesses.

How lucky they are. We who hate ourselves would give our left arms to join them in that sweet spot, that happy place, that sacred space. We would give anything. But that's the point. We at the low end of the spectrum believe that we have nothing to give.

Others might argue. Pointing out our talents, successes, and skills—our strengths—they would say: *What? Stop being silly. You have everything.*

We scoff.

We do not demand sky-high self-esteem. Just plain old medium will do. We need not hug ourselves. We need not bluster down the street singing our praises. This book is not about that, nor is it about drop-kicking our self-esteem from *low* to *high*. Instead, we seek only to stop stabbing ourselves. We seek the serene song of self-*respect*.

This book is about edging up to medium. Just there.

One of the best things about medium is that it frees one from thinking obsessively about oneself. Those at both extremes of the spectrum, ultra-high and ultra-low, translate everything into *me me me*. Dictators say: *Gaze upon me because I am glorious! I hate those sketchy people over there because they are inferior.* The self-hater says: *Shield your eyes upon encountering me because I am hideous! I hate those sketchy people over there because scorning them makes me feel slightly superior, but hmm, are my teeth yellower than theirs?*

Such tunnel vision, whether positive or negative, is boring, one-dimensional, and rude. Compulsively praising or punishing themselves, the self-absorbed see nothing but themselves. Getting to medium lets us be still, and look at something else.

This book is for all of us who languish between ultra-low and medium. This includes those with not so far to travel: those who do not hate themselves but do not like themselves, at least not much; that is, the moderately self-esteem-impaired, who wish they found it somewhat easier to dress and talk and eat and be alone and be with others and experience sheer joy. But this book is also for those with far to go, who genuinely hate themselves, who wish not just for whiter teeth but for faces they do not want to tear away in strips like orange peel. This book is for the desperate, who with every word and glance plead for permission to exist. You know the desperate, for whom life feels perfectly optional. The desperate, who wish not just for whiter teeth but also to be someone else, anyone else, please please, right now.

Introduction

Knock, knock!
Who's there?
Someone with low self-esteem.
Oh. Go the hell away, loser.
I knew you'd say that!

This silent epidemic makes nice, lovely, law-abiding people think themselves unbearable. It makes sweet, witty, friendly, pretty people slash their wrists. If you are reading this, you are probably one of us.

Cara, Nate, Rachel, Alison, Jeremy, Mariah, and me: On paper, we have everything, or nearly so. On paper, we are any or all of the following: Intelligent. Attractive. Solvent. Pleasant. Eloquent. Well-dressed. Well-traveled. Educated. Talented. Adored. On paper, we might have houses. Careers. Relationships. And yet we hate ourselves for complicated, often irrational-seeming reasons so unique to each of us that the outside world would not understand. The very notions of self-esteem or self-love are as alien to us as skydiving is to a barnacle.

We hesitate. We seethe in baseless shame. We lie. We talk, then tell ourselves *Shut up.* Some of us are the ones who call their cut-marks "battle scars." Our war is with ourselves.

We are the ones who overcompensate. We are the ones who stare into our closets every morning and think, *No no no, I cannot do this, not again,* but then, gritting our teeth, we do. But then again we feel as if we might as well not bother dressing, might as well walk naked down the street, because we feel *that* exposed anyway.

We are the ones who, when told *Have a nice day*, think: *What? Who are you talking to?*

We are the ones who sit and wait.

We are the ones who look away when cameras click. We are the ones who crash and burn, then crash and burn, then crash and burn, but no one sees.

We are our own constituency, our own clan. We could easily recognize each other on the subway, in the street, if only we made eye contact—but we do not.

We will not have a pride parade. We will not wear shirts that read *Hi! I Hate Myself!* We would be shocked to read our worldwide roll call and realize how many we comprise, a long and tragic line extending back through history. *What? You? And you? And you? Paul Cézanne, Abraham Lincoln, Michelangelo, Serena Williams—what are you guys doing here?*

What a bad thing to bond over. How shocking to consider ourselves a demographic. But for better or worse, you are not alone.

This is a book about being conjoined to—and occupied by—the very person you detest most in the world, someone who punches you in the face constantly and whispers horrors in your ears. Someone who talks you out of everything and trips you up when everyone is watching. Someone who sneaks up with a scalpel at the very second you start to have fun.

This someone waves your unwashed underwear in public, tricks you, and worsens your worst habits. This someone wants to kill you. This someone is you.

Self-loathing is a dark land studded with booby traps. Fumbling through its underbrush, we cannot see what our trouble actually is: that we are mistaken about ourselves. That we were told lies long ago that we, in love and loyalty and fear, believed.

Will we believe ourselves to death?

. . .

Our ancestors did not assess their self-esteem. Plowing fields, battling barbarians, they had no time to wonder: *Do I like myself?* Nor do members of some societies even today. For them, the very concept of how highly individuals regard themselves would seem a sacrilege and/or a silly luxury.

Self-esteem is a peculiarly American obsession and a fairly new concept in general. For most of human history, it went undiscussed. In nearly all cultures, the individual was less important than society as a whole. The individual was expected to roll with life's occasional highs and devastating lows and move on for the sake of the community. The individual was compelled to fit in, not stand out. Consider: Books have been written for four thousand years, since the *Epic of Gilgamesh,* but our literary forebearers rarely produced memoirs. And those who did were usually generals, adventurers, and conquerors describing deeds, not emotions—a far cry from most of today's navel-gazing autobiographers.

Mid-twentieth-century psychologist Abraham Maslow made self-esteem a cocktail-party topic by devising the hierarchy of needs, a pyramidal diagram charting the building blocks of well-being, with breathing and defecating at the bottom, morality at the tip-top, and self-esteem just under that. Maslow's contemporary, sociologist Morris Rosenberg, created the Rosenberg

self-esteem scale, which offers ten statements to be answered
with "agree" or "disagree":

*I feel that I am a person of worth, at least on an equal
plane with others.*

I feel that I have a number of good qualities.

All in all, I am inclined to feel that I am a failure.

I am able to do things as well as most other people.

I feel I do not have much to be proud of.

I take a positive attitude toward myself.

On the whole, I am satisfied with myself.

I wish I could have more respect for myself.

I certainly feel useless at times.

At times I think I am no good at all.

In practice, the Rosenberg scale is a little too obvious and blunt
to accurately "diagnose" people like us with complex self-
esteem issues. For example, after one quick look at the questions, I knew what they were trying to get at, then found myself
incapable of giving honest answers, instead giving answers I
thought would please the test-giver. Self-loathing can very clev-
erly confound attempts to assess it.

Self-esteem might be a fairly new concept, but professional
self-esteem hawkers are making up for lost time. Strolling

through an average crowd in America today, you would see evidence of a self-esteem glut.

In the 1980s, activists began promoting high self-esteem as a magic cure for crime, addiction, low test scores, and other social problems. This sparked a multibillion-dollar self-esteem industry that radically changed methods of parenting and teaching nationwide: Raising children's self-esteem was henceforth paramount. At school, in youth groups, and in many families, children were actually instructed to recite *I am perfect!*

Things have not turned out as planned. Studies reveal skyrocketing self-esteem among the young—but with none of those hoped-for reductions in addiction, crime, or other social woes. In fact, many recent studies link high self-esteem with *increased* aggression, narcissism, elitism, and racism.

So the self-esteem movement has not been universally successful. Many of its would be beneficiaries have fallen through the cracks, and just keep falling. Some of us were born too early to reap the movement's promised benefits: we were already grown up before self-esteem became an academic objective. But even many younger people who grew up in the alleged sunshine of the self-esteem movement have nonetheless suffered terribly. How can that be? Is it because the highly sensitive will always be highly sensitive in any environment—and the cruel and insecure and power-hungry, seeing that, will always pick on them? Has the self-esteem movement worked "too well" on *some* people, raising *their* self-esteem so sky-high that they feel justified in mistreating others?

A well-meant system designed chiefly to help those living under stressful conditions and great hardship and thus considered to be at high risk, the self-esteem movement has hardly been an overwhelming success. Clearly it has had the exact opposite of its desired effect on enormous numbers of young people. The steep rise in bullying and teen suicides is all the proof we need. Chanting *I am perfect* does not necessarily make one believe those words. Nor does it ease the solitary suffering of Zachary, who knows he will be called *fag* after class. Or Lily, who must go home to her stepfather no matter what. Or Morgan, every detail of whose life—straight As, sports, scholarships, success—has been planned in advance by loving relatives whose silent expectations clank like chains. Or Elle, who sees a monster when she looks in the mirror. Or Caleb, who wonders why the other kids never invite him to their birthday parties. Or Amanda, who finds scribbled on her locker the word *slut*.

Someone with high self-esteem, someone with low self-esteem, and someone with medium self-esteem are playing golf together. The golfer with high self-esteem swings, misses the ball, and shouts, "What an awesome swing!" The golfer with medium self-esteem swings, misses the ball, and says, "Oh well." The golfer with low self-esteem swings, hits a hole in one, and scoffs, "It was an accident! The wind blew it in!"

How did we lose it? No two self-loathing stories are alike. In this book we will hear some, but out there are millions more. Each is a kind of crime report, an epic tragedy. Yet most of these tragedies happened in private, behind closed doors, behind closed minds. Some in the outside world might call our traumas trivial. *Were you gang-raped? Sold into slavery? Imprisoned in a concentration camp? Did you accidentally tweet a naked picture of yourself to twenty million strangers? No? Then stop whining!* They would not understand that it is possible to be annihilated by a smirk, a scowl, an empty threat.

For thirty-seven-year-old linguist Kristy, it started in a suburban home. Her father was a noted neurosurgeon who cared about only one thing: achievement.

"But he had a very narrow view of what counts as achievement, in which the only three professions that count are medicine, law, and big business," Kristy remembers.

She continues: "My parents and my big sister talked to me as if I were stupid. They responded to the majority of my comments with derision and snideness, trying to find fault whenever possible—with my grammar, my logic, whatever. They made a sport of pouncing on my mistakes. At dinner almost every night, my father would join with my sister, teasing me until I got upset. Then he would make fun of me for being sensitive. My parents and sister assumed I knew nothing about anything, and they went into excruciating detail telling me what coat to wear, what road to take, what to say to people. There was an unwritten contract," she adds. "Both of my parents insisted that I be some kind of small person who did nothing but listen to them and agree with them and do what they told me to do.

"As I came of age sexually, my father acted in increasingly bizarre ways, assuming I'd gone from being a virgin to being a prostitute overnight. He had an unhealthy preoccupation with my body. I think he criticized almost every body part I have, and he often recommended plastic surgery. He was obsessed most of all with my weight. Most people don't think I have any kind of weight problem, but he sure did.

"Even when he wasn't making comments, I could feel that he was watching me, assessing me, judging me. Once when I was seventeen he said, 'Get up and turn around and let me see if you've gained weight.' I was shocked, but at the same time, I had sensed since I was six years old that that's what he was thinking about. To this day, I have a *lot* of trouble when people look at my body, even in clinical settings. When massage therapists and other types of bodyworkers try to assess my posture, alignment, and so on, I can barely tolerate it."

While studying Russian at college, Kristy took her father to a local Russian bookshop. In the shop, she asked the clerk a question in Russian. The clerk replied—in Russian.

"I was *so* excited," Kristy remembers. "I told my father that I had just asked for a book in Russian and that the clerk had understood me. My father said, 'Big deal. Can you ask for it in Dutch?'

"My father taught me all sorts of things about the world and especially about myself that I've had to unlearn."

. . .

The summer Ryan turned seven, his nineteen-year-old next-door neighbor, Kent, offered to babysit him every afternoon when Ryan's parents were at work.

"Kent told me we could play sports and watch TV,"

remembers Ryan, now a twenty-nine-year-old bar manager. "And we did—for the first week."

Then one day, while they were watching cartoons, Kent slid his hand inside Ryan's shorts.

"He put one hand over my mouth and said if I screamed no one would hear, which was probably true. He told me to relax and have fun."

It happened again and again on many afternoons over the rest of the summer. Ryan was too embarrassed to tell his parents. He thought they wouldn't believe him anyway. Kent was a straight-A college student, the pride of the neighborhood.

"I started third grade," Ryan remembers, "convinced that I was a gross freak."

. . .

For as long as she can remember, Sai didn't want to follow the life path expected of typical Laotian girls.

"I always knew I never wanted to marry a man and live with his parents and have kids," Sai says now. "I wanted to move out on my own as soon as I finished school, and start my own business—maybe even abroad. But I made the mistake of telling people this."

Her friends, relatives, and teachers were appalled.

"They all said, 'Good girls don't do that. If that's what you want, then you aren't a good girl.' I heard those words so often during my childhood that by the time I finished school, I believed them."

Once—somewhere, somehow, sometime—we were weak. Not helpless, necessarily. Not absolutely prone, just weaker than someone else at that moment, in that place, someone who seized advantage of that span, perhaps not even consciously. Whatever they said, we believed. Whether those words were spoken with malice or good intentions, aimed at us or overheard, the endgame was the same. If they said *Boys don't play with Barbies*, we believed them. If they said *You look fat in that*, we believed them. If they said *Your kind does not belong here* or *Why can't you go to Harvard/join the Air Force/be a ballerina like your perfect sibling*, we felt like failures. If they said *Shut up*—we did.

It was about body, brain, bank accounts, belonging, and belief. It happened all at once or bit by bit.

It could have happened anywhere along the line, but we were especially sensitive when we were very young, when all of life stretched out ahead of us; our brains were at their most impressionable, their most flexible, most keenly primed to learn.

It was a wicked spell. Whatever happened to you was a wicked spell.

Cara, Nate, Rachel, Jeremy, Alison, and me:

Today, one of us six writes TV scripts.

One leads a silent, scientific life.

Another attends weekly AA meetings.

One has left this world.

We who survived know what we have lost.

Alive and dead, we don't want company. We want us all set free.

Like most who are enchanted, we dismiss and deny our own histories. *Look how lucky you are*, we chide ourselves. *Move on.* But our stories, these incidents that made us hate ourselves, that thrust us into this volatile underbrush, are codes crucial to our recovery. Crack those codes and the lies all fall apart.

Someday we will escape our stories. We will walk out of them and away as we would walk out of a storm, a prison cell, a cinema showing a film we need no longer see, a store selling nothing we want or need. Right now our stories might still have something to teach us, might still contain clues. But someday we will walk away from here. Someday we will be free.

* * *

Here's a true self-loathing story. It goes on for a while, but only so that we can get to know each other. This book is not a memoir.

My mother shoplifts Tootsie Rolls.

I watch her do it as I trail her up the candy aisle at the Dollar Store. She told me, when we reached the store, *Don't follow me.* She did not say, *Because I want to steal.* She said, *Because we both want different things. You might need a new Rolodex.*

As if.

I dutifully walked away, then doubled back and shadowed her as she strode purposefully past Aisles 7 and 8, ignoring Smurfs gift wrap and panties printed with the words *Hello* and *So Much Fun.* Her slim arms swung, thin silver bangles bouncing. Rounding Aisle 9, partially shielded by a Twizzlers display, she stopped. I saw her slit open a bag of Skittles with a fingernail, pour some into her purse, and pop a few into her mouth. Glancing around, she tore open a bag of Tootsie Rolls. I watch her chew them now. As she does this, her businesslike eyes are hooded and stern as if she were working equations.

She need never steal. She could afford to buy all these candies and half the underpants as well. She could afford to buy a crate of gummy worms just as she could afford to buy prescription glasses instead of the dollar magnifiers she buys here. Whenever I say *See an eye doctor,* she says, *What could be worth that much money?* She means: *I'm not worth spending money on.*

The trouble is, I understand. I know exactly what she means. It does not puzzle me. She hates herself.

She hates herself because when she was very young, some people said (and quite possibly did) some things to her that filled her with great shame. I do not know entirely what it was, but she has not recovered. People now dead wrecked her life and thus nearly wrecked mine. I will not always hate myself, but on the day I watch Mom stealing Tootsie Rolls, oh heck yes I still do.

I hate myself because I am her child, her only child, a docile child born with what was then called a birth defect: shallow hip sockets. For five years I wore a steel brace that clanked as I watched Mom seize folds of her own skin while hissing at herself in the mirror *fat ugly pig.* Her fingernails made moon-shaped marks. She hates herself. I hate myself not because of the birth defect, which did not cripple me, but because in my brace days I knew my condition somehow made her sad. I hate myself because I cannot sing, because I cannot surf, because my mother hates herself: monkey see, monkey do.

Which finds me—at an age when some are surgeons,

professors, and admirals—trailing my mother in the Dollar Store. Whenever I come to Los Angeles, she always asks where we should go. *Museum?* No. *Zoo?* No. Because I know. This is her favorite place. It feels like home to her. I know.

It is late afternoon. This candy is the first food she has eaten since the day before. Whenever I arrive, she always tells me: *I already ate.* Night. Day. Ask what her meal was and she usually says fish. *Tilapia!* she lies. She starves herself between shifts at the gift shop where she volunteers, which has a candy drawer, and visits to the Dollar Store, where stolen candy does not count. She skips regular meals because this is a habit she adopted at age thirty-five, when sudden illness made her lose a lot of weight. Now that Dad has been dead for twenty years, she says she does not like eating alone, which I can understand. *No one,* she says, *ever invites me.*

She always asks her fellow volunteers, and everyone she meets, what they will eat next or just ate. *Grilled cheese,* someone might say. She listens, jaw working, as if engrossed in a fascinating film.

If I lived with her, I would scramble eggs and order Chinese takeout. We would face each other at her table. Her pear-shaped amber glass bowl would hold sliced fruit. Then she would eat. That much I could do but do not. Which makes her thievery my fault.

According to her rules, scrounged candy does not count as calories, as food. Whatever can be eaten without utensils, that leaves your hands clean, does not count. Nor does anything bite-size. In an ethereal sense, candy does not count because it tastes so good that it must be sent by God. Besides, my mother's father owned a candy store when she was six. Maybe candy reminds her of unconditional love.

Food eaten secretly remains exempt if no one sees you eat it. Like a tree falling in a forest with no one near enough to hear, Tootsie Rolls swallowed sub rosa could never make you fat.

I get this. I so get this.

My mother is intelligent, funny, worldly, dazzlingly kind to those in pain. She is the least racist, least homophobic person I have ever known. Self-hatred, however, renders her paranoid, hot-tempered, miserly. Self-hatred made us both think we are hideous, though we are not. Mom and I diverge. We both be-lieve we deserve to die. She wants to. I do not.

I seldom tell my husband anymore how scared of everything I am. Does anyone else think about leukemia while having sex?

I know this now: she meant no harm. She never knew how much a motionless, compliant child absorbs. She meant no harm to anyone besides herself. You might say this makes everything her fault. She could have gone to therapy. She could have read *I'm OK, You're OK*. She could have entered est. But no. So you could say, so I could say: *I know who killed me*. But I won't.

Our posture and eyes are dead giveaways, but she hides her self-loathing with bright clothes and jingly jewelry. I hide mine by being hard to see. I am so vague in every way as to be invis-ible. I make it a game: Acquaintances pass me on the street and in stores but never notice me. Inches away, they pass without a glance. Coworkers. Old friends, new friends. My first therapist. A relative by marriage, whom I'd known for thirty years. She passed. I shouted hello. Turning, she called me by someone else's name.

All this and more convinces me that I might not exist.

Not seeing me, Mom rips open a bag of Circus Peanuts. Extracting one, she presses its thick marshmallow softness to her palate with a moue of pleasure I can understand. Of course I can. She likes archaic candies—gumdrops, Smarties, Mike and Ikes—without realizing that they are artifacts, almost obsolete. She believes she is avant-garde because she went to NYU in 1949 and had gay friends in Greenwich Village who cooked in the nude. Yet she calls Sunday papers *the rotogravure* and all computers *that machine*. Someone gave her an iMac but she wept, banging the keyboard with her fists while sobbing *I'm stupid, I can't.*

She believes both that she is brilliant and an idiot, boring and interesting, elegant and crude, dirty and clean. This is low self-esteem. Confronting evidence of our magnificence, we still say *but.* I earned good grades in school but I am lazy and a space cadet. I never killed someone or even pistol-whipped them but I should wash my hair more.

And this (although I shouldn't tell you) is why you have a constant advantage over us who hate ourselves. Say something bad about us, even something you made up, and we believe you. We might not reveal it but you will have won, along with every bum who ever muttered *bitch* when I walked by. Your words will brand our bones.

We who hate ourselves always think we deserve punishment, God knows for what. No, literally. He does. Imagine how much worse it would be if we actually believed in Him.

Mom adores Circus Peanuts. Her eyes slide shut and she almost smiles. She is the nation's oldest anorexic. Like other addictions, other deprivations, anorexia springs from low self-esteem. I know because I spent years eating only almonds, dates, and one bagel a day.

One reason Mom likes visiting the Dollar Store is that it lets her leave her house.

Her friends think she is poor. A fellow volunteer named Genevieve and her son, Terry, bring my mother crates of Costco food. They think she cannot afford her own Costco food. I would laugh if this did not make me cry. Mom could eat every meal in restaurants if she so desired. And yet: *YOUR MOM IS H&U&N&G&R&Y!!!* Terry e-mails me, concerned for her, angry at me, both justifiably. *YOU DONT CARE IF SHE STARVES!!!???* Terry and Genevieve do not know that she stows their gifts away unopened. I find furred cheese in the fridge.

She will not eat. She will not read. She will not have parties or go to plays. But why? But why? But why? I know, and only I.

Which leads us here: to me idling beside the Almond Roca, believing I love her, which is why I would not tell the manager that someone is devouring Red Hots in Aisle 9. I watch her sharp cheekbones and large ears, believing I love her, which is why I would not shame her by exposing or confronting her. Any minute now, someone might.

Shoppers flow past. She turns her back to them and tucks her elbows in. The narcissism of the new America works in her favor as they pass her by oblivious, incurious, bent only on their Frosted Mini-Wheats and Clearasil.

Shoplifting candy—ripping, pouring, plucking, unwrapping—takes time. A bored or moral or observant passerby *might* be reporting Mom right now. Then she, who went to NYU, would gaze up to the sound of sirens and the click of cops' boots on the aisle. She would cry. I would cry. She would fling Circus Peanuts to the floor. Shoppers would *then* stare—because it would then be about them, spectators at an exhibition—as she sobbed, *I fuck everything up.* This is her song, the song of self-destruction.

Which is why, believing I love her, I must protect her. Which means stopping her. Which means starving her. Has she stolen enough candy to last one more day?

I bump into her as if accidentally.

Oh, there *you are,* I say.

She has two Circus Peanuts in one hand.

I brought these from home, she says. *In my purse.*

She pats the purse, looks at the Circus Peanuts as if wondering why she is holding them, then pushes them into her jacket pocket, which crackles like cellophane.

They sell nice candy here, I say. Discarded wrappers strew the aisle. At her feet is a plastic shopping basket containing two bags of colorful hard candies made in Mexico. These are meant for the gift shop where she volunteers. They are what justifies her visits to the Dollar Store. She always says, *We need refreshments at the shop.*

While packing for my trip two nights ago, I wrote the 23rd Psalm on the inside of a matchbook that I now keep in my wallet. As if I, for whom the Bible seems a weird agglomerate of garbled caveats and silly escapades, might suddenly be saved. It was part of an ersatz Self-Loathing 12-Step system I forged. *Step 8: List all the ways in which you've harmed yourself, and become willing to make amends to yourself for all of these.* The matchbook does not soothe me as Mom licks marshmallow from her teeth.

She looks around as if we are actually shopping.

Frowning at my empty basket, she says, *Surely you want something.*

No, I answer.

Come on. A lipstick?

No, because I never look in mirrors anymore.

Soda pop?

No, because I am a former anorexic.

Night-light? No. Because I am an adult and no longer afraid of the dark, but then again, a little glowing globe or elf or cat made in a Chinese factory would warm my heart more than the 23rd Psalm. But no. Yes. No.

Soap?

Why? I ask her. *Do I smell?*

We enter Aisle 10: cutlery.

Mom slides knives off the racks, eyeing the packaged ones and sliding the unpackaged ones along her hand. She does this with the smiling certainty of someone settling down to watch a favorite show. But I know she is gauging blades to see which would best slit her wrists. She does this every time but always balks. She asks me now, as always, *Will you forgive me if I do myself in?* What can you say? My friend Ellen committed suicide. Mom said Ellen was brave. Mom has asked me to murder her, not with a knife but with a pillow so she need not bleed. I always say no, but she asks and asks, the way you might pester a pal to paint your nails.

She sighs. We leave the knives and join a checkout line. I have a jar of olives in my basket. Behind us, two shrieking boys flog each other with pool toys while their mother adjusts her iPod and hums. Mom elbows me. We exchange looks. We who hate ourselves marvel at those whom we think should hate themselves but don't. The man ahead of us is buying charcoal briquettes. Mom asks him what he will barbecue.

Salmon, he says. But his eyes say, *Why are you asking me this? Why?*

I know, and only I.

· · ·

For more than forty years I believed I was not all there. For more than forty years I did not understand that I *was* there but someone else had made me believe I was not all there. That she had done this awful thing to me not on purpose but accidentally, because *she* believed *she* was not all there.

Which *she* was taught by someone *else*. Someone, sometime, somewhere back there in her small childhood world of beach bullies and schoolyard taunts had told her lies. And that was her enchantment.

It became a competition: Which of us could hate herself the most? This felt perversely safe to me. If we kept this up, she would neither hate nor fear nor be angry at me for leaving her behind. If we maintained this understanding, she would feel less hated somehow and maybe more loved.

And thus, dawn after dawn, the boxing glove. The fist.

But hey. I never see it anymore. Well, almost never. As you

read this book, you'll notice that I sometimes describe my self-loathing in the present tense and sometimes in the past. *Which is it?* you might ask. *Are you better or not? Or are you just a sloppy writer?* If only it were that easy. Sometimes it feels like the present, sometimes like the past. Let's just say I am *making progress.* That is all I ask of you. If I have clawed my way this far, then you can too.

No one-size-fits-all ritual will break the code for all of us. No two paths are quite alike. But some of them are *definitely leading out of here.*

I don't know you, but I would wager that, in all your life, you have done little harm—except to your own self.

Start here: You are astounding just for being human, merely for belonging to this species that is capable of language, laughter, creativity, and love. With just one hand, you could soothe a child, play a tune, or stitch a wound. With just one eye, you could signal warning or friendship, read the entire contents of a library, or find your way out of the woods. And your brain is the universe's greatest creation.

You might be unready and/or unwilling to hear even this primordial paean right now.

Prepare for future paeans, but I promise I will never ask you to smile into mirrors and say you are sexy. I will never ask you to chant affirmations or make Republic of Me flags for yourself, emblazoned with a picture of your face.

I *will* ask you to stop hating yourself. How much is up to you. But *pssst,* even a little less self-loathing is a lot.

What a difference a day without boxing gloves makes.

CHAPTER 1

You Were Not Born with Low Self-Esteem

*The greatest hazard of all, losing one's self, can occur
very quietly in the world, as if it were nothing at all. No other
loss can occur so quietly; any other loss—an arm, a leg,
money, a wife, etc.—is sure to be noticed.*

—SØREN KIERKEGAARD

Come to the drinking fountain with me, Tammy says, or I
will never play with you again.

We are six. The bell marking the end of recess has just rung,
and a trip to the drinking fountain would make us late to class.
Tammy is always saying such things, Do this or that or I will
never play with you again. She says them in a reasonable voice
as if to say, *You know, you* could *refuse, ha-ha.*

In my plaid skirt under that vast blue sky I suddenly feel
hollow, like an avocado shell scooped clean. *Do what she says,* I
think, not in words but electric jolts. Another child—a braver,

more secure child—in this situation would have scoffed at Tammy: *ha*.

But Tammy is my best friend. If I refuse to go with her to the drinking fountain, she might really never play with me again. And why should she? Tammy has other options. Tammy is a normal girl. No one makes fun of her as they make fun of me. Why does she ever even play with me at all?

This hollow feeling did not start with Tammy but at home, where Dad sometimes yells at me right out of the blue: *goddamn you*. Home, where Mom laments, *Whatever I touch turns to shit*, which saddens me, since (a) my mother cannot lie, and (b) in giving birth to me, she touched me. QED. In our tract house with its cactus garden, hi-fi, and long hallways, Dad hollers, *Goddamn you*. He is brilliant. He would know.

Like all six-year-olds striving to make sense of the world, I take words at face value. When Dad's frayed patience drives him to shout *goddamn you* at me, I take it literally and picture God processing Dad's request. When Mom says everything she touches turns to shit, I believe her just as I do when she tells me snowballs are cold. She likes to boast that she never talked baby talk to me because I am so smart, because I can converse like an adult. I can, but only in the imitative sense, as in playing pretend. She speaks freely to me as to a fellow grown-up. Pretending to understand, wired to learn, I take each word as fact.

Okay, I say, then follow Tammy to the fountain. We make it to class with two seconds to spare. No damage done. Or so you say.

That true story contains no violence. No beatings, molestations, or guns. Yet thinking of it, having lived it, makes me feel hollow again. And terrified. *Tammy might never play with me again.*

Which would be my fault. As is everything.

We who hate ourselves came to hate ourselves in many different ways. For some, it was the big stuff. Guns and blood, the kind of trauma you can see. For others, it was little things: Laughs. Glances. Words said or unsaid. Your self-loathing might have begun with something so seemingly slight that even speaking of it, even saying what it was, makes you ashamed because society, this grown-up world beset by tidal waves and wars, might scoff: *how insignificant.*

And yet however trivial, however large or small or loud or silent, it occurred. And nothing was ever the same again.

Tammy saved my life, as best friends do, many times before and after that day. Her idle threat did not destroy me. It was just a tiny chisel nicking one more tiny fragment from my crumbling sense of self, another proof that I was not one who made rules. I was one who said *I'm sorry* and *Yes.*

And Tammy, with her amber eyes, knew almost none of this but never doubted that I would comply.

• • •

POP QUIZ

Do you think everything that goes wrong is your fault?

Do you replay every past conversation in your head, regretting everything you said?

*When anyone is nice to you, do you assume they're joking
or that this is part of some devious scheme?*

Do you apologize compulsively?

Do you occasionally feel invisible?

*Do you sometimes think all the wrong people have all the
self-esteem?*

Hello, friend. Welcome aboard!

You weren't born this way.

No creature ever was.

There was a time before you hated yourself.

How long did it last?

Developmental psychologists say that this pre-self-loathing period, this span of perfect if unwitting peace that is the biological
birthright of every human child, lasts for at least the first three
years of life. Developmental psychologists say that human infant brains are neurochemically and psychologically incapable
of the kind of self-reflection that can warp into self-loathing until age three. Before age three, the human brain is bent entirely
on survival. It cannot yet find fault with itself. In a technical,
cellular sense, this is self-love.

Human newborns are far more helpless than newborns of
other species. Ducklings hatch already knowing how to swim.
Horses, deer, and other hoofed creatures take their first steps
mere hours after birth. Dragonflies emerge from the water in

which they were hatched already knowing how to fly, hover, *and* devour prey in flight. Compared to such precocial species, which are born already equipped with all the skills they will ever need, Homo sapiens is altricial: born ignorant and almost totally defenseless, gaining skills very gradually while being protected by adults. Altricial species have much larger brains than precocial species, and are capable of learning much more —eventually.

Newborn babies never question their existence. Like infants of all species, they have but one desire: *to keep existing.* Infants do not perceive their demands as demands, just as *life.*

Newborn babies experience emotions. Very soon after birth, they start expressing happiness, surprise, anger, and fear. To some extent, they think. In one study, whose purpose was to determine whether young babies can choose to modulate their behavior in order to produce pleasurable results, a group of two-month-olds were shown that they could hear musical tones if they sucked hard enough on specially outfitted pacifiers, but that if they did not suck hard enough, they would produce no such tones. The babies consistently chose to produce musical tones.

Babies become aware during their first year that their bodies occupy volume, that their bodies are separate from other objects, that the movements of their bodies can impact other objects, and that their bodies are capable of mimicking the actions of those other objects. This knowledge gives babies what psychologists call an implicit sense of self—the self merely as an object in space. But at that age all emotions, all experiences, are forgotten almost immediately after they pass. At that age, science tells us, all memory is short-term memory.

But even in its first two years, while doubling in size, the rapidly growing human brain is rapidly learning to please. In one study, eighteen-month-old babies watched as adults responded to various foods with happy or disgusted faces. Asked to select some of the foods to give the adults, the babies consistently gave the adults whichever foods had made the adults appear happy.

By age two, toddlers can recognize themselves in mirrors. A full sense of self emerges in toddlerhood, as children first register their physical *and* mental states—pain, opinions, plans—as belonging to themselves, not to others. At this age, they first feel ownership, use first-person pronouns, and savor their first sparks of agency: *It's mine.*

Long-term memory begins at around age two, as the brain masters words and symbols and the neural circuits connecting the frontal cortex and hippocampus mature sufficiently to store experiences for more than a few minutes at a time. In one study, researchers played games with a group of nine-month-old babies and a group of twenty-month-old babies. Revisited four months later, the first group retained no memory of the games. The second group remembered them well.

By age three, self-awareness deepens as children start understanding themselves to be what developmental psychologists call "enduring entities"—individuals whose past and present experiences intersect and have meaning: *I spilled the milk, just like before, which made Dad mad.*

At age three, two new emotions—embarrassment and shame—appear for the first time. At three, children begin reacting to their mirror images by sometimes turning away or hiding their faces. Thus begins the dawning of the social self, the public self, the seen self, the judgable self.

That is, the self that can hate itself.

With this dawning comes a terrible risk: that the newfound capacity for self-assessment can go the wrong way, that the first assessment will be: *I am bad.*

Once that assessment sticks, we're stuck. We become "people with low self-esteem." Ask us why we have low self-esteem and each of us will rattle off long lists of mental and physical flaws. Is some of this "evidence" accurate? Of course. No one is perfect. Damage happens. But try this trick. Think of certain people you despise. They have done or still do things you would never do. Rape. Arson. Despotism. Dropping litter on the sidewalk. Yet some such people love themselves. We hear self-love in their words and see it in their eyes. If they are capable of even average self-respect, then so are you. Perspective, people. Do the math. How many houses have you robbed today?

Self-loathing is something we *do* because it is something we *have.* This doesn't mean it's necessary, merited, or permanent. You can call self-loathing a sickness if you like, but you could just as rightly call it a condition, a delusion, a persuasion, or a dream. We weren't born this way. Let's not die this way.

Easier said than done, you argue. Yes, it's hard. We have to fight self-loathing every single day. It is a sneaky monster that follows us everywhere, padding behind us silently only to jump us when we are most vulnerable and whenever we feel nearly happy or safe. This monster has been with us for so long, has been our one constant companion for so long, that we believe it and trust it, more than we believe or trust new friends. Our task now is to kill this monster, not just placate it or drown out its roars with beer and other distractions as we have done for so long but slay it, blow by blow and hour by hour.

Because, I ask you, what purpose does self-loathing serve? We're on Earth for such a short time. How do we want to spend these years? In pain? Blinded by hatred? Paralyzed by fear? By what gauge could this conceivably be okay? Is the pain of self-loathing somehow more endurable, more socially acceptable, than the pain of being impaled? Is self-hatred less stupid, less a sin, than hating others? Is fear of our failure less traumatic, does it merit less compassion, than fear felt during a flood or war? The difference between *our* pain, fear, and loathing and those other kinds is that we are at both the giving and receiving ends. To stop hating ourselves is to reduce the quantity of pain and fear and loathing in this world.

But yes, it's hard. One of the self-fulfilling prophecies about self-loathing is how infantile it makes us feel: how helpless, how arrested, requiring a steady stream of reassurance.

With all our fears and insecurities, we crave encouragement and comfort but are virtually incapable of giving these things to ourselves—because *we* are the very ones we fear, the ones who make us insecure. *We* are the ones we trust the least. *We* are the ones we've been running from. We might as well seek reassurance from Don Rickles or the Big Bad Wolf.

We who hate ourselves are bottomless pits of need. If people really do avoid us, this is why: because they have lost patience with our ask-ask-asking for acceptance, for approval, for for-giveness, for permission to exist. They say, *I told you everything was fine a thousand times, thus clearly (a) you do not respect my opinion, (b) you are totally self-absorbed, and (c) you'll just keep asking me.* They call us addicts, and we are.

Because our unplumbed need is one more thing we hate and fear about ourselves, it muzzles us. We stop asking for help and, facing what we call a terrifying world, we lash ourselves to masts.

Conventional science says that no matter what happened to us before age three we were safe from self-loathing, *incapable* of self-loathing, because before age three our brains were not able to store memories for more than a minute or two. But not every-one agrees with conventional science. Some theorists believe that self-loathing can begin as soon as we emerge from the womb.

Mid-twentieth-century British psychiatrist John Bowlby in-troduced a new idea that he named "attachment theory," in which new mothers can doom their babies—often unwittingly—to lifelong self-loathing with their own negative facial expressions, body language, or tones of voice. According to Bowlby, "disor-dered attachments" need not entail obvious abuse: to ruin ba-bies' lives, new mothers or other early caregivers need only appear distracted, distant, depressed, angry, impatient, ex-hausted, or ill. They need only be absent for extended periods of time, and/or overcompensate for their own distress by acting overprotective or expressing exaggerated, implausible "pseudo affection"—that is, cuddling too much.

"The infant and young child should experience a warm, intimate, and continuous relationship with his mother (or permanent mother substitute) in which both find satisfaction and enjoyment," Bowlby wrote—*or else.*

Similar ideas were vaunted by Swiss psychotherapist J. Konrad Stettbacher, whose "primal therapy" program guided adults to trace their self-loathing back to babyhood. According to Stettbacher, a newborn in the "primal stage" of life has "primal needs": food, warmth, and comfort.

"When those *primal needs* are not met," Stettbacher warned, "a child will become unsure of itself. If its tears or calls for help go unheeded, it will increasingly become a helpless prey to fear and pain. Unfortunately, the child will interpret this [fear and pain] as a product of *its own* inadequacy." In Stettbacher's view, newborns who cannot yet speak or contemplate will *blame themselves* for their own hunger, cold, and discomfort if their cries go unanswered for too long, if their mothers look sad or ill or act inconsistently—cuddly one hour, cold the next:

"If the infant could talk, it might say something like this: '*I'm* incapable of making myself feel more comfortable. *I* am too weak. *I* can't manage it,'" Stettbacher wrote.

Occurring before long-term memory develops, this preverbal, precognitive, primal-stage self-blame imprints on its tiny victims an unarticulated pain that makes them feel, for the rest of their lives, as if they have "always known" that they were "deficient . . . worthless or bad," Stettbacher theorized.

"If we have been traumatized in this way, we will, in later life, fall into patterns of reaction set off by certain key features and signals. . . . Though we will not be conscious of it, the stress arising from such a situation will constantly make us feel it, like an unhealed wound," creating a "permanent feeling of unease."

These theories are interesting, especially for those who cannot trace their low self-esteem to any remembered incident. Are Stettbacher and Bowlby correct? Could some loving, caring adult have triggered your self-loathing unwittingly by looking sad one day?

My earliest memory finds me being lifted from my crib. Sunlight slants through the bamboo curtain of my turquoise-blue bedroom. My grandmother, tall and strong and red-lipsticked and businesslike, not your gingham pastoral type, has been tasked with changing my diaper. Struggling with some phase of this process, Grandma sighs. *Oh beans.* This is her customary oath, the phrase she substitutes for cussing. Did I know this then? Or was her tone of voice, a surliness that mocked the pillow-puff of *Oh* and rendered *beans* stiff as a stick, enough?

Oh beans. Grandma sighed from the whirring, perfumed, sunstruck heights, and lying there I must have known that something was upsetting her: my diaper or its contents or the room, some vector of badness circling back to *me*.

Okay, so we weren't born with low self-esteem.

Maybe conventional science is correct in stating that we can't start hating ourselves until we're three.

Or maybe Bowlby, Stettbacher, and their ilk are correct in stating that we can start hating ourselves far earlier.

In either case, at some point after being born—be it three days, three years, thirteen years, sixty—certain people start disliking themselves. Who? What does it take? Surely it could happen to anyone. But are some of us neurochemically pre-destined, biologically more likely, to dislike ourselves? Although no baby is born hating itself, are some babies born predisposed to low self-esteem? Could a low self-esteem gene exist in our DNA?

Under identical circumstances, all else being the same, three randomly chosen children are told that they are ugly and stupid. Two won't believe it. One will. Why?

Scientists have identified a breast-cancer gene, a diabetes gene, an obesity gene, even an addiction gene—and have actually come close to identifying a self-loathing gene.

In one study, researchers set out to determine whether variants of the oxytocin receptor (aka OXTR) gene might be linked to psychological aspects including self-esteem, optimism, and a sense of mastery. Popularly known as the feel-good hormone, oxytocin is a hormone linked with positive emotions and social skills. The researchers found that people who had one or two copies of the OXTR gene with a type of allele known as an adenine allele tended to have less optimism, self-esteem, and sense of mastery—and more negative emotions such as depression—than people who had a different allele known as the guanine allele.

Human beings *aren't* all born alike. Our personalities,

potentialities, and latent likes and dislikes were to some extent blueprinted in the womb—largely by genes.

This is a relatively new discovery. For most of history, it was assumed—even by great thinkers, from Aristotle to Freud and beyond—that human beings are blank slates at birth: all identically uninflected, our characters coalescing over time, shaped wholly by our families, circumstances, and societies—that is, by nurture, not by nature.

Recent research shatters this tabula rasa theory. Magnetic resonance imaging reveals highly varied, highly individualized patternings and concentrations of gray matter—which comprises mainly neurons and synapses—in the brains of human newborns. These diverse patterns have been shown to prove that many traits and talents are inborn.

Studies of twins are further evidence. Gray-matter patterns in the brains of identical twins, who share 100 percent of their DNA, are far more similar than gray-matter patterns in the brains of fraternal twins, who share only 50 percent of their DNA. Gray-matter patterns among randomly selected, unrelated human pairs are vastly dissimilar.

These variances "are not just differences in anatomy, like the shape of your earlobes. They have consequences in thought and behavior," according to leading brain researcher Steven Pinker.

"We're not born blank slates. Kids come into the world with certain temperaments and talents. It doesn't come from outside."

Again, twins provide evidence. In the Minnesota Twin

Family Study, thousands of twins who had been separated at birth or soon afterward and were raised apart as strangers were reunited as adults and compared. One such pair comprised Oskar, raised in Germany as a Nazi-sympathizing Catholic, and Jack, raised in Trinidad as a practicing Jew.

Reunited as adults, Jack and Oskar displayed amazing similarities. Both habitually wore rubber bands around their wrists. Both flushed toilets before *and* after using them. Both liked dunking buttered toast in coffee. Both even enjoyed sneezing in crowded elevators.

Oskar and Jack *must have been* born with these highly individualized traits. Although gray matter can fluctuate over a lifetime based on experience, the chances of both men having independently adopted such unusual habits while being raised as strangers half a world apart are nearly nil. The Minnesota study yielded a wealth of similarly amazing cases.

"Something is written on the slate," Pinker asserts.

Just as some people are born with aptitudes for math or music and with preferences for rock-climbing or bowling, and just as some people are born debaters or born sailors, those with the putative low self-esteem gene are born with innate sensitivities that establish them as born self-haters. They don't hate themselves at the literal moment of birth any more than born debaters are literally born debating. But if the low self-esteem gene really exists, born self-haters are perpetually at higher risk than other people for losing self-esteem, just as those with family histories of diabetes and cancer are at higher risk for developing those diseases.

Which traits might the low self-esteem gene entail? Studies have not yet been conducted examining the MRIs of newborns for the long-term purpose of gauging and tracking their self-esteem. But if gray-matter patterns can predetermine toilet-flushing habits as it did for twins Oskar and Jack, then gray-matter patterns can predict propensities for shame, fear, pessimism, insecurity, hypersensitivity, perfectionism, self-absorption, doubt, and other esteem-crushers.

According to one biographer, Franz Kafka's lifelong struggle with low self-esteem was due to his "highly developed capacity for seeing himself in the eyes of others." Was he born this way? Would brain scans have revealed in the newborn Kafka an extreme hypersensitivity to being judged?

The painter Paul Cézanne reacted so strongly to criticism that while still young he earned the nickname *l'Écorché*, meaning "the flayed one." It was the name of a sculpture of which he owned a cast, and which he drew again and again—fascinated by the metaphor of a skinless man. Did Cézanne's gray matter preordain him to be not merely thin-skinned but virtually skinless?

You don't *need* the self-loathing gene to hate yourself. But, if it exists, it helps.

But genes are no guarantee. Someone *with* the low self-esteem gene could be born into a gentle, supportive, nonjudgmental family and thenceforth by a great stroke of good fortune encounter only gentle, supportive, and nonjudgmental people—in every playroom, classroom, club, workplace, and street. Perpetually buffered, this lucky person—despite being at-risk—might never develop low self-esteem. Then again, someone *lacking* the low self-esteem gene could undergo a trauma and be lost.

Nature and nurture conspire to shape our self-image. The possible existence of a low self-esteem gene is liberating in the same sense that it is liberating to learn that people with epilepsy aren't possessed by demons. The possible existence of a low self-esteem gene lends scientific heft to the notion of self-loathing as a syndrome, an assemblage of molecules that could happen to anyone.

Examining the nurture side of our self-loathing stories liberates us too. Sifting through memories, seeking sparks in the dark, we ask: *How did I get this way?* Each anecdote is evidence. With it, we shout: *Eureka. Now I know.*

But sooner or later, we have to ask: *Does it even matter anymore?* However we got here, we all share a goal. This is our path, our practice: to stop hating ourselves. Starting now.

. . .

It is the first day of the Girl Scout Camporee. Twenty-five troops from all over Los Angeles have set up tents beside the sea. I am an only child and naturally solitary, which is why Mom—who is neither of those things—enrolls me in so many group activities: to make me sociable, she says.

She has also enrolled me in a guitar class, art classes, drama classes, day camps, and a Jewish youth group that folk-dances in the park.

It's good to learn music and art. It's good to learn camping and crafting and life-saving skills. Drama might come in handy someday. But. Learning these things *this* way, jostled by jeering kids, is brutal for a loner like me. Had I ever been told *You are a solitary type, it's who you are, a lot of people are this way, including famous brilliant ones, and it's okay,* my self-esteem might be intact. But I have never heard any such thing. Instead, I have always been watched—worriedly, angrily—by parents, teachers, counselors who dislike the fact that I like to play alone. Sometimes they ask if I am sick. Sometimes they ask why I refuse to share. Sometimes they seat me next to social kids who make me want to disappear.

And every team on which I am the last child chosen, every dance I spoil by being out of step, every giggling clique that points at me and laughs lowers my self-esteem because even while selling myself out, I fail. I should not care what others think of me, but in a crowded world, insults can sear. Every new group activity is one more forced ordeal of inauthenticity, anxiety, pretense, and self-denial.

Allowed to learn some of these camping-crafting-dancing skills alone, or with a tutor or my father or my best friend, would have had the opposite effect, making me not just skilled but proud and confident. After twelve years of group activities, I can crochet and play arpeggios and pitch tents and make tourniquets. I also hate my hands, my hair, my feet, my face, my voice—especially when singing or starting to cry.

Preparing for the Camporee, hoping to earn arts-and-crafts badges, I have made myself a halter top out of a red, folded-in-half bandanna and a string. I have also cut and sewn the seat of my old Levi's into a purse, adding a leather strap. Wearing my halter top and purse with cutoff shorts, I cross the parking lot to meet my troop. I know these girls from school. None of them are my friends. The first girl giggles. Then the next.

Someone raided the garbage can, she says.

Can't she afford to buy real stuff at stores? another asks.

Yes, but that's not the point is what I am thinking but cannot say because I cannot speak because—my voice, my awful voice—I am starting to cry.

Wook! She's cwying! someone says in a baby voice as laughter mingles with the boom and swash of surf.

And I know it is nothing. It is, yet is not. And I am thinking: *Shut up, you imbecile crybaby!*, wanting to tear my top and purse off and throw them into the sea. As it happened, I never wore either of them again.

It was the small things and I always thought: *Never again,* but it always happened again. And again. That was it: the next small thing and then the next, those tiny cuts. Now those moments seem smaller still, remote and minuscule down the train tracks of time, which just makes my remembered pain all the more ludicrous compared to that of those who survived beatings or abandonment or rape. Compared to them, compared to nearly everyone, I was the lucky one. Compared to nearly everyone, I have no right to write this book.

Or don't I? Does it really matter how you or I lost our self-esteem? Are some self-loathing stories more worthy of empathy than others? Do some sources of self-loathing count more than the rest? Does some judge say, *Compared to Jeff, whose father beat him with a baseball bat, and Zia, who was forced into marriage at five, your so-called traumas—short legs! mean Girl Scouts!—were trivial. You are a dilettante. Go home.*

Are those who lost their self-esteem by accident less quali-
fied to be here than the brutalized? Are size-8s who wish they
were size-2s, silver medalists who wanted gold, and loners who
were forced to folk-dance simply poseurs? Is this charted on
some diagram? Are some of us disqualified from some grand
Pageant of the Sad? Must we compete, even in this?

And must we simply shut up because *some* people out there
in *awful* circumstances smile and carry on? That man has no
arms. Look, a homeless child. Refugees who lost everything.
Their self-esteem is fine. So get. Over. Yourself.

No. Okay, yes. But in a good way. So, no. All of us who hate
ourselves have the same right to be here. All of us have level
places at this table, equal voices in this dialogue. No hierarchy
divides us. Pain is pain, however it begins.

And however you got here, one thing is for sure: your self-
loathing is not your fault.

. . .

I call self-loathing *autophobia*, fear of the self.

This is the greatest fear of all, fear of the one thing we cannot escape: our bodies, minds, and lives. At five I knew already
that I had no power in this world except the dumb involuntary
power to be ugly, stupid, fat, disgusting, mockable, rejected,
wrong. I had no power but the unwitting reflexive power to get
hurt or sick, to be abducted, killed, to fail and make my parents
mourn. I had the power to possess ugly hair, ugly freckles, ugly
feet. I had the terrifying power to choose friends, which was
really the power to choose those who would betray me or might

die, because whatever power I had was the power to lose every-thing I loved.

The power of those who hate themselves is the power to be powerless. We try to be good, well, attractive, and alive. But at age five, I knew my mind and body were both my worst ene-mies and they were always waiting, pulsing, to humiliate and hurt and kill me. Think you're safe in that cute checkered shirt with its red tulip appliqué, safe from the itchy shiver of dread as the camera clicks? You're not.

And this was our apprenticeship: learning to fear our every move.

And find no refuge from our fears, because what we feared most *was always there.*

Which made us hide from ourselves. Starve ourselves. Kill ourselves, obviously. Dose ourselves with substances by which we could not recognize ourselves. Cocaine as camouflage.

And walk around in fogs.

Come out. Come out.

. . .

However your self-loathing started, chances are it started very long ago.

"Some of us," wrote the heiress and fashion designer Gloria Vanderbilt, "are born with a sense of loss. . . . It is already there from the beginning, and it pervades us throughout our lives. . . .

"Loss, defined as deprivation, can be interpreted as being born into a world that does not include a nurturing mother and father."

Vanderbilt's multimillionaire father died when she was a baby. Her socialite mother showed scant interest in parenting.

"We are captured in an unbreakable glass bubble, undetected by others, and are forever seeking ways to break out, for if we can, surely we will find and touch that which we are missing," Vanderbilt wrote. "I hope you don't live in this invisible glass bubble, but if you do I am one of you. I know it well, and as the years passed, I sometimes recognized it in the eyes of strangers and sometimes in the eyes of those I loved, and when it was not there I rejoiced."

Before she was a world-famous actress envied and desired by millions, Kate Winslet was a 5'7", 180-pound schoolgirl. Her classmates called her "Blubber" and repeatedly told her that, because of her size, no one would ever find her attractive.

"Even now I do not consider myself to be some kind of great, sexy beauty. Absolutely not," Winslet said in 2009, after winning an Academy Award.

That such famous and wealthy women suffered this way would surprise many. But money can't buy self-esteem.

Nor can anything else. Self-esteem might be the world's most precious commodity. We enter this life soft and helpless, strangers to everyone, *including ourselves*. Henceforth, we remain largely at the mercy of this world and its inhabitants. Here our troubles begin.

The survival instinct, that most basic and elemental of urges, starts at birth. For most creatures, it persists unquestioned, unremitting, until death. But something strange happened to you and me and Gloria Vanderbilt and Kate Winslet and millions more that changed all this. It happened in our infancies or afterward. It happened because of genetics or because of human interaction or by accident or by some combination of all three. It happened with a jolt, or bit by bit. It happened because, as human beings, all of us were and are at risk.

The human species is unlike all others: vastly more intelligent, equipped with language, logic, and incomparable skills. Chief among these skills are our methods of communication, modes by which we tell each other how to feel. Beavers slap their tails on the water to announce approaching danger. Civets mark their territory, warning others off, with dung. We humans have developed subtler ways.

Our species is the only one that kills its own for sport. The only one that puts such stock in its own thoughts. Is our species also unique in that its members steal each other's self-esteem? Not quite. Lions, elk, and seals sparring at the start of mating season hope to become leaders of the pack, leaving losers to cower, bleeding and humiliated, in the wings. But in this skill as in so many others, Homo sapiens have transcended the basic, brutal, eye-gouging *I win* to craft ingenious upper-end modalities achieving the identical effect: asserting power, crushing spirits, striking fear. In our exquisite brilliance, we have elevated the art of humiliation.

Our species is cruel in ways that no other species can match. We have mastered not just humiliation but also manipulation, competition, deception, seduction. Human beings invented airplanes and aspirin, but we have also invented ten thousand kinds of guilt.

Dogs don't do to each other what we do. Ravens would never dream of it.

"Just as soon as children develop awareness, it is essential to demonstrate to them by word and deed that they must submit," advised Swiss philosopher Johann Georg Sulzer in his 1748 *Essay on the Education and Instruction of Children,* a text not atypical of its type and time.

"It is impossible to reason with young children," Sulzer asserted. "Thus, willfulness must be driven out in a methodical manner. It is quite natural for the child's soul to want to have a will of its own. . . . One of the advantages of these early years is that force and compulsion can be used. Over the years, children forget everything that happened to them in early childhood. If their wills can be broken at this time, they will never remember afterwards that they had a will."

Of course, it is not always parents who steal self-esteem.

"I had very loving parents," says my forty-five-year-old lawyer friend Bettina. "But I was the girl all the boys at school barked at and called a dog. I would come home crying my eyes out and there was nothing my mom and dad could do to make me feel better. All I had to do was look in the mirror and I would remember the boys going 'Arf, arf' and I would think they were right.

"That's why, when I was a sophomore in college and someone took a liking to me, I was astounded. When he asked me to move in with him, of course I said yes. When he turned out to be a sadistic jerk, I thought I deserved it. I kept remembering those boys saying 'Arf.' It took me years to get away."

Who did it? Who stole your self-esteem? It could have been anyone.

Biracial actress Halle Berry says she was "shunned" at her

all-African-American elementary school after her classmates learned that her mother was white:

"Overnight, I didn't fit in anymore."

After changing schools, Berry was the only child of African-American heritage on her new campus. Racist indignities ensued: Oreo cookies stuffed into her locker. A white principal who accused Berry of having cheated her way to prom queendom.

"I always had to prove myself through my actions," Berry recalls. "Be a cheerleader. Be class president. Be the editor of the newspaper."

The trauma left marks. Although millions admire her talent and beauty, Berry warns: "Just because they see my face doesn't mean they see me. . . . Self-esteem comes from who you have in your life. How you were raised. What you struggled with as a child."

Shannon Lambert was fifteen when she was raped by an acquaintance at a friend's home after a high-school party.

"I remember just clinging to the metal on the bed and looking out the window and feeling like I was dying," Lambert said four years later on TV's *20/20*. "Then he finished, and he patted me on my head. . . .

"I got up and took a shower," remembers Lambert, who later founded the rape-victim support network Pandora's Project. "And it all settled in while I was taking that shower. . . . I thought I must be a dirty, horrible person if this happened to me. And I was trying to wash it away. But it wouldn't go away."

From childhood through the teen years, the human brain is

undergoing rapid development but remains "under construction." Certain brain regions—such as the dorsolateral prefrontal cortex, which is just above the temples and largely responsible for planning, impulse control, and the discernment between lies and truth—do not reach their full adult level of functioning until we reach our twenties or even thirties.

Young brains are neurochemically wired to stay open because in those early years they have so much to learn. But one of the things young brains can learn is how to hate themselves.

At some point, *something* stole our self-esteem. And suddenly the strongest, most primeval instinct in the world, the survival instinct, became a question mark. At that point, we learned this strange trick, self-loathing, this perversion, just as we learned to subtract, play chess, or eat with forks. Maybe no one directly told us we were worthless, but we came to that conclusion anyway as the only rational explanation of how we were treated or how we felt.

And once young brains learn languages, real or metaphorical, they're hard to forget. Once self-loathing becomes entrenched, it feels like identity. Its harsh words sound to us like our own native tongues. Its pain feels as natural, autonomic, and necessary as breathing. And once self-loathing feels normal, it's a kind of addiction—a strange enslavement that offers none of the thrills or comfort that drugs, sex, and alcohol do. Once our grown-up brains have "learned" self-loathing, then unlearning self-loathing, breaking that addiction, requires serious commitment, work, and time: the slow recircuitry of how we actually think.

In a sense, this is why meditation was invented. Deeming desire and hatred "the afflictive emotions" that trap people in a cycle of birth, aging, sickness, and death and thus spur suffering, the Buddha devised a method of mental discipline aimed at raising self-awareness and seeking the harmonious "middle path" between these two extreme emotions. The hatred that the Buddha found so "afflictive" is, in our case, hatred of ourselves. The "middle path" is not so different from the resilient midpoint on our self-esteem spectrum.

The spiritual teacher Eckhart Tolle says that problems with self-image start when "you believe in every thought that arises. . . . Why do you have a low view of yourself? Because you believe in your thoughts. And why are you thinking those thoughts? You picked them up somewhere, maybe in your childhood. Maybe your mum was so stressed-out that she said, 'You're no good.'"

Negative thoughts "get stuck in your head and refuse to go, and the more you believe in them the more deeply lodged they become," says Tolle, who describes people with low self-esteem as being "stuck with hostile, life-denying, continuously critical and attacking entities that they carry in their heads and they believe . . . and they are constantly attacking themselves, or if they are not attacking themselves, they attack others around them."

When we were taught to think this way, we lost our baseline belief in our right to live. We lost that sensibility, which is a given for every blue jay, flatworm, and whale. Where did it go?

It went. It was taken from us. Stolen. By so-called friends, by family, by society, by strangers, by those who bathed us in their hate or falsely claimed to offer love. It was taken from us by those who aimed to cripple us or meant no harm. It was taken from us by illness, injury, or accident but almost always because of our fellow human beings, it went.

. . .

The good news is that the you you hate is not the real you.

We all had a "time before." Not all of us remember it. Joel, a sixty-one-year-old airline executive, has photographs of his "time before." He recognizes the house, the yard, and the people in these pictures. But he can't remember smiling into the camera lens. He can't remember being the happy baby in those pictures. His memories begin only in second grade, when his father began beating him with belts and his mother began burning him with hot frying pans and curling irons while his younger siblings watched.

"I have seen pictures that were taken of me between the ages of eighteen months and three years in which there is a smile on my face. But not after that," Joel says.

"I have no memory of ever having any kind of mind-set except the self-hatred that still plagues me. I have no memories that are happy. The verbal, emotional, and physical assaults came with such ferocity that it was a chore—no, a full-time job—for me to be on the lookout for the next one."

Joel can't remember his "time before," but Ava can. The thirty-eight-year-old studio musician used to perform live at clubs but is grateful that her current work keeps her out of the public eye.

"I used to love to be photographed. I used to love being the center of attention. I used to be confident and secure in myself and I used to feel really great all the time."

Ava's "time before" lasted throughout her childhood and teen years, through college and early adulthood as she began a promising career onstage. Then she met a certain someone.

"In our nearly nine-year relationship, he was perpetually looking for something else, for someone else. I was lucky if he had sex with me even once every three months. He developed a serious porn addiction, and it was all about the skinny girls. If you're constantly being compared to waifish, stick-thin eighteen-year-olds and you're over thirty, nearly six feet tall, and a size eight, not a size zero, what can you do?

"I slowly stripped away all that made me happy in order to stay in a relationship that left me an empty shell," Ava remembers, "like the kind you see buried in the sand at the beach and get all excited about but then discover that three-fourths of it is missing and it's not the perfect memento you were hoping for."

Ava knows *how* and *when* she learned to hate herself. She knows *who* taught her. She can pinpoint moments in that learning process. Bit by bit, day by day, for nearly nine years: she knows how she got to Self-Loathing Land but *not* how to get back across that underbrush, how to get back to who she was, how to pick up where she left off *before*.

She is one step ahead of some of us, because she knows she must get back. She knows she *had* a "time before." She can remember its shapes, sounds, and silhouettes. She still knows people she knew then. They can be witnesses. She has their memories and hers. She is lucky in that.

Reconnect with your "time before." Try to remember it. What were its bright landmarks? What did you love?

Revisiting your "time before" is not the same as dwelling on the past, stuck in reverse. Revisiting your "time before"—leapfrogging backward over your self-loathing years—is a valiant return to your true self, your innocent and trusting self, which has been waiting for you back there all along.

Our true selves are the selves we were before we twisted, bent, and beat ourselves into the shapes we had to take in order to please others: the shapes that we hate. Our true selves are the selves we would have been had no one tried to break or shame or change us. Our true selves are what those who actually love us see in us. Our true selves are who we have always been, even if they have been in hiding all this time. Our true selves are who we will, in that sheer blue zone above self-loathing, always be.

Our true selves are the selves we do not hate. Revisiting our "times before"—to remember, refresh, restore, rebuild, rejoice, and reconnect—is going home. From which our true selves never left. Where we can start again.

We *can* go back.

But first, we must believe.

Knowing what we now know about the human brain and how it grows, that we entered this world *not* hating ourselves, thirsty to learn, we must believe this:

Learning how to hate ourselves was merely one of countless things we *could* have learned. In those same hours we have devoted to self-loathing, we could have learned how to play the flute or repair clocks instead. The same brainpower we have poured into self-cutting, say, or anorexia could have been spent attending sailing school or inventing fluorescent toothpaste. But it was not.

Of all the potential lessons in the world, self-loathing was just one. It was by random, tragic, potentially fatal accident that we found ourselves enrolled in Self-Loathing 101. In it, we learned: Have fear. Lose heart.

Thusly ended our "times before."

And yet what has been learned can be unlearned.

Genetics, happenstance, and human interaction worked their will on us. And yet:

The latest research reveals that, thanks to a phenomenon known as neuroplasticity, human brains can be continually retrained all throughout life. This process is never again as easy as in childhood. It takes longer to learn foreign languages at forty than at four. But they can be learned at forty, sixty, or eighty nonetheless. And scientific studies show that even a few minutes of daily mindfulness meditation or concentration can literally change the way we think and feel on a long-term basis, transforming chronic negative emotions into chronic positive ones.

And what is self-loathing if not a constellation of negative emotions such as fear, shame, dread, regret, self-criticism, hyper-vigilance, anxiety, depression, sorrow, and rage? And where did these emotions start in us? With some horrible trauma, or ten thousand tiny hurts—offenses or insults, meant or unmeant?

Buddhist teacher Pema Chödrön tells us that in the Tibetan language, those tiny hurts are called *shenpa,* which she defines as "getting hooked."

"Someone criticizes you. They criticize your work or your

appearance or your child. At moments like that, what is it you feel? It has a familiar taste in your mouth, it has a familiar smell. Once you begin to notice it, you feel like this experience has been happening forever. . . . Even a spot on your new sweater can take you there. At the subtlest level, we feel a tightening, a tensing, a sense of closing down. Then we feel a sense of withdrawing, not wanting to be where we are. That's the hooked quality. That tight feeling has the power to hook us into self-denigration. . . .

"Shenpa is usually involuntary and it gets right to the root of why we suffer. Someone looks at us in a certain way, or we hear a certain song, we smell a certain smell, we walk into a certain room and *boom*. The feeling has nothing to do with the present, and nevertheless, there it is."

It isn't easy, but we can learn to resist and renunciate shenpa.

"If we can see shenpa just as we're starting to close down, when we feel the tightening, there's the possibility of catching the urge to do the habitual thing, and not doing it," Chödrön says. Resisting any habit, even a painful one, is hard. "The urge is so strong, the hook so sharp, the habitual pattern so sticky" that "unless we equate refraining with loving-kindness and friendliness toward ourselves, refraining feels like putting on a straitjacket."

Tell yourself: *I'm doing this for your own good.* This time, it's true.

We can change our brains, but it takes time and diligence, because the human brain has a built-in "negativity bias" whereby it stores and learns from negative experiences far more readily and lastingly than it stores and learns from positive ones. This is a natural survival strategy by which the body records danger signs for future reference. It is far more useful for an evolving creature to remember *Hungry lions bite* than to remember *Flowers are pretty.* Thus we are neurologically wired to remember more vividly and lastingly a bad experience—say, a public scolding—than to remember a good experience—say, hitting a home run—that occurred on the same day, even if both experiences carried exactly the same emotional intensity for us at the time.

"The brain is very 'sticky' for negative preoccupations," neuropsychologist Rick Hanson told me. "It's like Velcro or a super-sponge for the negative and Teflon for the positive. That negativity bias worked great for our prehistoric ancestors who lived short lives and had to survive under harsh conditions. For us in the modern world with our longevity, anxieties, and self-criticism, the negativity bias is a serious challenge. If you rest your mind upon a lot of crap, that's what will stick to it.

"Mental activity requires neural activity; neural activity sculpts neural structure," said Hanson, founder of the Wellspring Institute for Neuroscience and Contemplative Wisdom and author of *Buddha's Brain: The Practical Neuroscience of Happiness, Love, and Wisdom.* Because new neurons are forming constantly, he says, "changes in the mind associated with changes in the neural system leave lasting traces in the structure of the brain. Neurons that fire together wire together. Mental states become neural traits."

Hanson compares the human mind to a wet washcloth in that it "takes the shape of whatever it rests upon. If you routinely rest your mind on self-criticism, anger, or anxious rumination, your mind will take a negative shape. Alternatively, if you routinely rest your mind on positive, constructive emotions, it will take on a positive shape."

A growing number of studies confirm this. In one such study, magnetic resonance images revealed that even eight weeks of daily mindfulness-meditation sessions created a "positive shape"—mainly characterized by structural changes in the hippocampus that calm down the brain's alarm system and reduce its reactiveness to stimuli that previously triggered negative emotions.

In or out of a spiritual context, meditation is the process of learning to refocus attention, "and that's the absolute foundation of resculpting the brain," Hanson said. "What's fantastic about this is that it's never too late."

Adopting meditation as a healing practice can be a spiritual quest or as pragmatic as joining a gym. No cushions, gongs, or bells are required (although, granted, there are apps for that). Even mini-meditations scattered throughout the day can help. Pausing for a brief bit of undisturbed silence, spent in non-judgmental non-thought, simply observing the moment, might feel strange, especially at first. But which would you rather learn: serenity or ten new ways to hate yourself? Granted, the fact that we learned how to hate ourselves through pain and trauma makes unlearning harder. In unlearning how to hate ourselves, we must acknowledge that pain, then move on—just as you would acknowledge the barbs in barbed wire when climbing through to safety on the other side.

Make neuroplasticity work for you. Set out to learn something. *Anything.* It could be something easy or something hard.

It could be something done with others or alone. It need only be something you desire to master, do, or know. Thai cooking. First aid. Astrophysics. Hackysack. This practice occupies your mind, derails its default urge. Self-loathing is an action, driven by a craving as intense as any thirst on Earth, an impulse nearly irresistible, as if thinking of anything but our own flaws is dangerous.

Give that energy something else to do. Give it a *project*, although at first this makes you feel like a fugitive. And whatever you choose to learn, you will also at first of course tell yourself that it is worthless, ridiculous, and/or impossible. But you are making a heroic shift: transforming from someone with low self-esteem into someone with a quest.

And almost *whatever* you learn will make the world a better place. Keep some sign of it near you always. Whenever self-loathing swells, reach for that wrench or manual or microscope.

Adopting quests reshapes our thoughts from negative to positive, retrains them to link effort and anticipation and reward. And learning is its *own* reward. The bonus prize is a new skill, a quantifiable accomplishment.

I have done this myself. Granted, I interspersed my quests with starving and wanting to leap in front of speeding cars. But memorizing Chinese verbs healed ragged wounds, and now I can make shiny jewelry out of silver wire.

You might not, *and you need not,* ever love yourself. You might not, and you need not, ever call yourself Genius, Gorgeous, or Fabulous. You might not, and you need not, ever call yourself anything nice at all. Just stop calling yourself bad words. Put down the razor blade. Resist. Refrain. Is that so much to ask? The greatest gift you can give yourself is to, now and then, stop thinking of yourself. Each inch is exponential sweet relief.

Many of us learned our bad "lessons" the hard way. Joel did. The words his parents said when they were beating him with belts and burning him with frying pans stayed in his head long after he had left their house. Those words stayed in his head when he went off to war, came home, married, had kids, divorced, married again, divorced again. Those words stayed in his head with every drink he took, long after those who said those words were dead.

Dust somewhere, they still speak.

Their words were never true. Joel never was a "crazy useless wise-ass brat." His true self, left back in his "time before," was a dreamer who loved to read about faraway places as he sat beside a creek, singing when nobody was listening, fashioning leaves and sticks into boats, whistling as they sailed.

What did they call you that you weren't? What did they never say about you that you were?

. . .

It happened once upon a time.

On that day, you were innocent. Both in the sense of having done no wrong and in the sense of not yet knowing evil, you were innocent.

You required something from others and/or society, or you were told you did. Was this thing you required acceptance? Safety? Love? Someone, or several someones, saw your need.

And in their cruelty or their madness or their blindness or their insecurity, maybe meaning no harm, they said or did the wrong thing to a trusting soul.

That was the moment of enchantment.

How could you know, in your innocence, that everything was soon to change? That words, looks, gestures, human interactions could turn into wicked spells? That right then, right there, one was cast?

A blackout. Fitful sleep. Then you were on your feet. They did not feel so steady as before. They never would again.

Your true self—your self from the "time before," your pre-self-loathing self—was not killed in this spell but left suspended, spun in silk, inert like Sleeping Beauty and Snow White, potentially forever, while the self that was allowed to join the world was your self-loathing self, which looked like you and had enough humanity to pass for you, even *to* you. Your self-loathing self staggered off not knowing, not remembering: simply hating itself.

Your flesh felt unfamiliar: Partial. Strange. Scooped out. Your spellcaster or spellcasters were nowhere to be seen.

We who had once sat minding our own business were thereafter doomed to wonder, always wonder: not as we had wondered in our innocence, forever asking angel-softly why boats floated and the sky was blue, but with a terrible new kind of doubt that burned like lye.

We hated ourselves. And we would never know anything for sure again.

Especially about ourselves. From that point on, we never

knew whose whim would dictate our next move. We could never discern whether what we were told, or what we said ourselves, was truth or lies. We never knew how we appeared to others: okay or grotesque. We never knew whether others desired or hated us, or how they would feel about us five minutes hence. We never knew how hard to try. We never knew what we deserved. We never knew why pleasure felt like pain.

I call this the Uncertainty Curse.

In its thrall, we never knew what we would wreck next, just that it would be something, soon. We never knew whose voices we heard in our heads saying bad things. Sometimes it sounded like our spellcasters, sometimes like us.

We never knew.

We might remember what happened to end our "times before," but not the crucial part: that it had been a spell.

In the state of unknowing, the Land of Self-Loathing, we wandered, feeling strange in our flesh and wobbly on our feet, our eyes never quite clear, guessing and second-guessing, always half-suspecting that the words *Kick Me* had been secretly tattooed on our backs. Our never knowing made us do strange things we thought might maybe, possibly, miraculously make life seem more certain to us, might relieve that endless nausea of never knowing. We did alien things we would never have done in the "time before," transforming ourselves in our desperation into exponentially ever more bizarre versions of ourselves. What must I say, do, or be now to evade anger, punishment, humiliation, pain, or shame? What must I wear, eat, drink, or take? I will do anything, even if *anything* means nothing. Then

I would say nothing, do nothing, think nothing, feel nothing, eat nothing, and become almost invisible, practically vanishing into thin air.

The Uncertainty Curse is like having all your doors and windows wedged and painted open, and you cannot pull them shut. Meanwhile, your flies are always open, your buttons undone. Nothing is ever finished in your mind because you turn it over and over. Any question anyone might ask? The truth is, you don't know.

Pretending certainty becomes the tragic mission of your life. You find yourself at age fifteen or twenty-one or thirty with no choice: Everyone else your age is growing up, finding themselves. Yet you have been denied this dream, this evolutionary charge, this physiological reflex. Acquire tools for discerning the truth? Decide what you believe in? Learn to trust your hunches? No, not you.

This is your curse, and it will taunt you, trick you, tear you limb from limb. Imagine nothing coming easily. Imagine nothing ever feeling true. Even when your gut says it's true, your cursed soul never knows, never allows itself to know.

In our not-knowing, we recited scripts our spellcasters had made us memorize. We wore costumes we hoped would hide our awfulness. A uniform alleging our allegiance to whatever we believed would make us pass for normal, for acceptable, for lovable, for anything but us. Disguises. Because we no longer knew. We had been told things about ourselves that changed everything.

Keisha, now a forty-two-year-old stay-at-home mom, was

never teased about the large keloid scar on her chest until the first day of seventh grade.

"Before that, it was always hidden under my clothes. My parents and sister had never made a big deal out of it. But in seventh grade, we started having to dress for gym and take showers in a locker room. The other girls all started pointing at my scar and screaming 'Mutant!' and 'Beware of the blob!' and I just stood there wanting to disappear down the metal drain in the floor. I had never felt freakish or deformed before that, and I can go for days without feeling that way now. But sometimes it suddenly comes back to me, even when I'm fully dressed. Even though no one can see the scar, I just want to run somewhere and hide."

How can we break the spell, when we walk this world believing not that we have been mesmerized, not that we were cursed into autopilot, not that we were merely told that we are bad *but that we actually are bad?*

We say: *He left me because I am bad. These trousers don't fit because I am bad. The waiter was rude to me because I am bad. I can't think of anything to say to this person next to me because I am bad. I did not get into Yale because I am bad. I want another doughnut because I am bad.*

It goes deeper and deeper, until the spell that started it all becomes a distant incident, merely one of a million moments demonstrating what we now believe is true: that we are bad.

And then it doesn't matter anymore how many teachers, coaches, friends, and strangers say that you are good at this and great at that. It doesn't matter because you can't believe them.

The fix is in.

• • • •

Often the circumstances in which we lost our self-esteem were relationships distinguished by a steeply unequal power balance.

Our spellcasters were parents. Teachers. Bullies. So-called friends. Strangers. Romantic partners. Cliques. Coworkers. Your spellcaster was the mean first grader. Or the psycho in the dark. Or the town, school, Scout troop, spiritual community, family, neighborhood that did not understand your type, whatever that type was. Your spellcaster could even be society at large, that nameless, faceless "them" with boundless power and a thousand biases.

And it became unbearable to be the bullied one, the hounded one, the outcast and excluded one. *If you can't beat 'em, join 'em,* the old saying goes. Others hated us, or appeared to. We joined 'em.

Most of us had no choice but to submit. A baby cannot pack his bags and move away from his irresponsible parents. A friendless child cannot magically produce pals out of thin air. A girl born into a misogynistic culture will still be a girl. A beaten spouse might keep on being beaten for decades, believing that the sole alternative is poverty or lifelong loneliness.

We wanted food, love, company, support.

Which is to say, we wanted to survive.

And much of what battered us had nothing to do with us. We were the vessels into which others hurled their frustration, shame, and rage. We were the clear mirrors of *their* self-loathing, *their* sickness, *their* autophobia. We were just hapless passersby, consumers, and observers.

And as others—individuals or institutions—wielded power over us, we lost autonomy, lost agency. We shrank. We disappeared. We gave ourselves away.

Psychoanalysts call this process "soul murder."

"Soul murder is neither a diagnosis nor a condition. It is a dramatic term for circumstances that eventuate in crime—the deliberate attempt to eradicate or compromise the separate identity of another person," wrote psychoanalyst Leonard Shengold in his landmark book on the subject.

"The victims of soul murder remain in large part possessed by another, their souls in bondage to someone else. . . . Brainwashing makes it possible to suppress what has happened and the terrible feelings evoked by the erased or discounted experiences. When it is necessary to retreat from feelings, good feelings as well as bad ones are compromised. . . . Therefore murdering someone's soul means depriving the victim of the ability to feel joy and love. . . .

"Torture and deprivation under conditions of complete dependency have elicited a terrible and terrifying combination of helplessness and rage: unbearable feelings that must be suppressed for the victim to survive. . . . Soul murder is as old as human history, as old as the abuse of the helpless in any group."

"You trade your reality for a role," said Jim Morrison in a 1969 interview. "You trade in your senses for an act. You give up your ability to feel, and in exchange, put on a mask."

In Henrik Ibsen's 1879 play *A Doll's House*, long-suffering housewife Nora tells her overbearing, narcissistic husband, Torvald, that he is one of her soul-murderers:

"When I was at home with Papa, he told me his opinion

about everything, and so I had the same opinions; and if I differed from him I concealed the fact, because he would not have liked it. He called me his doll child, and he played with me just as I used to play with my dolls. And when I came to live with you . . . I was simply transferred from Papa's hands to yours. You arranged everything according to your taste, and so I got the same tastes as you—or else I pretended to," Nora explains.

And whose tastes were they really: his or hers?

"I am really not quite sure. . . . I have existed merely to perform tricks for you, Torvald. . . . You and Papa have committed a great sin against me," Nora rages. "It is your fault that I have made nothing of my life."

Ibsen revisited soul murder in a later play, *John Gabriel Borkman*.

"You are a murderer!" one character shrieks at the man who deserted her. "You have committed the one mortal sin! . . . You have killed the love-life in me. . . . That is the double murder you have committed! The murder of your own soul and of mine!"

Bent on survival, brainwashed, striving to suppress our fear and frustration and rage, some of us bought into myths about the relationships that stole our self-esteem. In the 1950s, pioneering family therapist Don deAvila Jackson introduced the notion of "family homeostasis," in which dysfunctional families firmly resist change. Such a family, Jackson wrote, is "a closed information system" that strives to maintain a status quo by creating "family contracts," in which it is understood that each member must play a certain role—for instance, the youngest sibling is pegged as the golden child, the eldest as the problem child, and the middle sibling as the peacemaker. These contracts operate in accordance with family myths, in which all members of a family conspire to perceive and convey a whitewashed version of the truth.

Daniel, a forty-two-year-old restaurateur, witnessed how such contracts and myths played out in the family of his childhood best friend, Tim:

"Tim's parents idolized his older brother Kevin, who in their eyes could do no wrong. Tim was born last—an accident, I believe. His parents resented him from day one. Anytime anything went wrong in their house, Tim was blamed. If a dollar went missing, Tim stole it. If the goldfish died, Tim killed it. If a cup got chipped in the sink, Tim broke it.

"But I was with Tim the whole time. He was always innocent. Meanwhile, Kevin knew *he* could misbehave all he wanted just so long as he could foist the blame onto Tim if his crimes came to light. Kevin became more and more evil, knowing he'd always get off scot-free. Sometimes he'd even frame Tim just for the sheer sadistic pleasure of it.

"By the time we reached high school, Tim had become a total basket case. He had internalized the role assigned to him and began to truly believe that he was always guilty. Since he was being blamed for everything, he decided that he might as well do the crime since he was already doing the time. He became a delinquent, and we drifted apart. Odds are he's in prison right now. He became the bad guy his family expected him to be."

How much nicer it sounds, how much more normal one feels when one says, as Joel did in his youth, *My mother bakes the best cakes in the world* than to say *My mother burned marks into my back with red-hot pans.*

The first sentence sounds *so* much nicer. We repeated such sentences like affirmations until we believed them. Someone who bakes great cakes can't be crazy, mean, or bad, can she?

We who hate ourselves scrambled for scraps. We forgave wrongs so speedily, so totally, for so long as to wipe those wrongs from history. Whatever pain we perceived we ascribed to our own flaws.

Myths are nice while they last. We can expand Jackson's concept to include clique myths, workplace myths, and other myths. To smash the myths, to think that we could or should have fought back, to think about how badly we were tricked, to calculate the waste, would just make us hate ourselves more.

. . .

I am closing my locker at the gym when a girl using a nearby locker touches my charm bracelet, recognizes the shapes of its chunky charms, and says, *Babylonian ziggurats! My favorite type of ziggurat!*

I turn and smile, a split second too late, because the girl, who looks about fifteen, has withdrawn and flattened her back against the wall as if expecting to be slapped.

Sorry, she says wetly through the braces on her teeth, eyeliner-circled eyes clear and intelligent. *I talk too much.* Her hair is long, greasy, and straight, one lock dyed tangerine and braided for display but so tightly that it jerks like a wire. Around us, other girls her age are grinning into mirrors as if being filmed, drawling in those loud, overhear-me voices girls now use: confident girls, not girls like *her*.

One slender hand flies to her mouth. She wears two rings made from bent nails. A red X is scrawled on her thumb.

No, hey, I say. *That's perfectly okay.*

She laughs as you would if told you were the pope. As if to say: *Yeah, right.*

And we are strangers but I want to rush her out of here, take her someplace where she can smile, where she can dance through fragrant fields, talk as much as she likes, and be at peace. Someplace safe. I want to say: *I know, little girl. I know.*

She blinks like someone clinging to the sharp edge of a cliff. But I just say *bye-bye* and leave. Later I think I should have given her my bracelet. At least that. Should have, but too late now. Too late.

People like us can recognize each other if our eyes meet. *Take these broken wings and learn to fly.*

Groucho Marx once said that he didn't want to belong to any club that would have someone like him as a member. We can all relate.

None of us joined the Self-Loathing League on purpose, for fun. We are the Accidental Demographic, an unwitting and unwilling subculture that does not know its own dimensions. Gazing at those we believe are beautiful, successful, calm, and confident, we do not recognize our fellow sufferers as such. Are *they* surprised to see *us* here? Might even the least sociable among us seize the nearest hand and spread the whisper down the line: *Welcome. We are all leaving here. Together. And at long last, you belong.*

Roll call:

Forty-year-old bank manager Jenna can pinpoint exactly when she first felt her self-esteem draining away.

"It was the moment when I was twelve and my mother said, 'You would be so beautiful if you just lost some weight.' This absolutely came out of nowhere. When I look back at pictures of myself from that time, when she said that to me, I can see that I was not at all a big girl.

"My mother had always wanted to be a ballerina. My elder sister studied ballet and had a dancer's body. My mother was expecting that to happen to me, but it didn't. I didn't do ballet. I didn't have that kind of body. I swam. I played basketball. I did rough-and-tumble things. I didn't do the feminine, delicate things that give you long, lean muscles. Plus I physically took after my dad, who has a bigger frame.

"But after she said that, at that moment—that's when I became extraordinarily conscious of my body and very miserable about it. I started dressing differently—in big, manly flannels and big, baggy trousers. Those kinds of clothes were fashionable then, in the grunge era, but I probably took it further than I should have. I remember being judged by my mother for every single thing I put into my mouth. To this day, I have a very unhealthy relationship with food. I have an eating disorder; not in that I am anorexic or bulimic—I'm not—but in the sense that I feel extremely guilty every time I eat anything that isn't water. Of course I have body issues."

Invited to spend the weekend with her new boyfriend's family on their houseboat, twenty-two-year-old office worker Miya was so afraid of sounding stupid in front of all these well-educated people that she hardly said a word. They tried to draw her into conversations, asking what she thought of everything from tidal charts to yams. But whatever they asked her, Miya shrugged and rolled her eyes. After a day of this, she overheard her boyfriend's sister asking him: "Is Miya shy—or just a stuck-up bitch?"

"Sometimes I don't feel as if I'm a person at all. I'm just a collection of other people's ideas," David Bowie told an interviewer in 1972, the same year he scored pop superstardom with his iconic Ziggy Stardust persona. Twenty years later, Bowie confessed that while filling auditoriums with impassioned fans back then, "I had enormous self-image problems and very low self-esteem, which I hid behind obsessive writing and performing. . . . I was driven to get through life very quickly. . . . I really felt so utterly inadequate. I thought the work"—songwriting, recording, performing—"was the only thing of value."

I was one of those who were tortured by accident by those who meant no harm.

My parents yelled a lot.

Not in the sense of talking loudly to show enthusiasm, as one might when discussing politics or art. Not in the sense of talking loudly to be heard over a din at football games and jolly restaurants, but outraged *yelling*, with flushed skin and throbbing veins and bulging eyes, the way you might do to an arsonist whom you saw setting fire to your house, but they did it to me.

They did not want to yell. They did not plan to yell. They were well-meaning. Educated. Open-minded. Married for eight years happily childless, they were pressured—it was then the social norm—to have a child. They loved me. They did everything for me. I know this and am grateful. Mom had been a Manhattan department store executive. That was the only circumstance that had ever made her feel proud, confident, competent. She loved her glamorous, prestigious, demanding career. She traded it for me.

When I was old enough to crawl but did not crawl, she took me to the doctor, who discovered that my pelvis had only the shallowest of hip sockets. Without medical intervention, I would be disabled for life. I was promptly fitted with a steel brace, versions of which I wore for the next four years. This process resulted in hip sockets that then allowed me to walk almost normally.

Mom loathed herself and nearly always had, but hid this from the outside world. In public she was businesslike and competent. In private she scowled at her mirror image, calling herself *Pig* and *Hog* and *Elephant*. Sometimes she cried, and I would have done anything to help her stop, to take the pain away. She stayed up nights, afraid my brace would fail and that I would remain a lifelong cripple, mocked by passersby. When we were out together during my brace years, she scowled at strangers whom she thought were staring at her child.

Mom mourned. She had produced a broken thing, which she believed was typical of her and all her fault. And yes, although I was the loved one, the protected one, I was also the one who made her mad, because I could, because I was a child, because I was the everything-she-touched-that-turned-to-shit. When I was not a baby anymore but old enough to be disorganized and leave things scattered on my bedroom floor, she sometimes stood there in the doorway, shrieking: *You're a fucking slob! Like me!*

Although I was the one she fed, the one in whose pockets she placed notes saying *I love you,* the one for whom she wanted all good things, she yelled. Why? Because she hated herself, and my existence made her feel afraid and presented a thousand daily opportunities for her to feel incompetent. Why did she hate herself? Why would a statuesque NYU graduate with a devoted husband, ranch-style house, and daring and eclectic taste in clothes and objets d'art hate herself?

Was it because something bad happened to her long ago about which I was never told? Was it because those playground bullies called her *Fatty Fatty Four-by-Four?* And/or was it because (I would wager) she was afflicted with borderline personality disorder (BPD), whose symptoms she heartbreakingly displayed: explosive rage, relentless fear, social anxiety, black-and-white thinking, mood swings, eating disorders, smooth public self, chaotic private one, self-loathing, suicidal tendencies. Most people with BPD never seek treatment (because they believe they deserve their pain) and thus are never diagnosed. Come on, you would yell, too.

Dad was an optimist. He had grown up poor and fatherless, but happy. He had served in World War II. Now he designed communications satellites while his wife anguished over their imperfect child. Nothing distracted her from dread—not faith, not steak, not sense, not a sun-dappled patio. She was impossible to reassure.

What choice had he? He would not leave us. That was that. But he could yell. Yelling at each other was useless, as they both yelled back. Yelling at me, however, brought relief because I would stare up at them, horrified, and then cry.

Their anger could erupt at any moment, without warning, often (you might argue) without cause. *Your friends are fucking bitches! Your room is a sty! How dare you speak in slang!* The unpredictability was the worst part of it. That and the loudness. And the words.

And deep down, had I not been in a state of shock, I might have thought: *What the hell did I ever do to you?*

But no. It never crossed my mind that adults could *choose not* to yell. I reasoned that if someone old enough to have a job and wear a suit and drive a car screamed at me, I deserved their rage. I must.

One night when I was ten, Dad handed me a paper cup full of shelled peanuts to hold as he drove. I did not want to spill them but they spilled. Dad pulled into a parking space, leaped from the driver's seat, scooped peanuts from the floorboard, and flung them theatrically into the air. Nuts rained onto the pavement. Dad stomped them into a paste under his shoes while passersby stared and he railed at me: *Goddamnsonofabitchbastard.*

One night when I was fifteen he picked Tammy and me up after a high-school football game. I spent the ride home composing alternate lyrics for top-forty songs. *M-m-m-many tourniquets,* I sang instead of *Bennie and the Jets.* Tammy laughed and laughed. Dad dropped her off, then whirled on me and yelled: *Are you her jester now? Her goddamn clown?*

I came to understand that I was always making someone mad. Or could. That I gave them no choice.

Such knowledge makes you sit perfectly still by day and grind your teeth to powder as you sleep.

· · ·

I learned words: *Don't. Die. Dangerous.* Mom showed me the sandblasted circle on our corner where a car had crushed a neighbor boy. She came into my room and sat on my bed every night and bade me to tell her everything I had done that day which she had not seen or heard. I told. *I baked brownies with Mandy and her mommy. We jumped rope.* She listened, sharp shoulders outlined against the wall. *Oh God. How many brownies did you eat? What did they think of you? After you left, did they call you a pig? Did Mandy's mother go to college? Jumping rope is dangerous! What if you fell and broke your teeth?*

I thought all children told their mothers everything—at least, all girls. Whatever I experienced all day I knew that I would later tell her. She would analyze it, then tell me what to think and what to fear. And it was all for my own good. Despite her daily agony, she gave me art supplies. She taught me how to be polite. What else in the world could this be but love?

Other girls had un-anxious mothers—carefree smiling shrugging mothers who said, *Grin and bear it!* and *Look on the bright side!* and *Tomorrow is another day!* Mom gave me her terrors as you might bequeath pearls. *Her* urban childhood terrors—*Fatty Fatty Four-by-Four*—flashed in *my* sinewy sub-urban flesh and screened like filmstrips in *my* eyes. Since my own TV dinner days, my fears were hers, then mine, and thus nothing to do with me but everything.

She taught me what she thought.

Fear food, she said (because it makes us fat). Fear hugs (because whoever hugs us feels our fat). Fear school (because they grade you, and make you play volleyball). Fear females (sneaky sluts) and males (because!) and time (because it passes) and talking (you can take nothing back) and animals (germs), rain (accidents), and whomever is not related to you by blood.

A car is not a car, she said while driving to the mall. A car is not a steel box but a lethal weapon, two tons of potential death for you and those whom you could carelessly destroy, those whom with one flick of the wrist you might run down or crush like canned goods in *their* cars. Imagine their intestines spool-ing swiftly on the blue upholstery before it catches fire. And you, behind the wheel, out for an errand or a merry spin with, say, your children or best friend and they would see it all. Per-haps the crash could kill them too and of course you.

A friend is not a friend, she said, but merely he or she who stabs you in the back. Yes, just you wait. The blade slips be-tween your ribs silently, then twists. A friend is not a friend but he or she who, when you weep, waits with his or her arms out-stretched, knife up one sleeve, laughing at your naiveté, think-ing, *What a sweet setup! Three, two, one, touché.*

She called my red-haired best friend the Red Devil, not in jest, as in *cute li'l devil*, but literally, privately, only to me: *The*

Red Devil tells everyone you're weird. I want to strangle the Red Devil. The Red Devil just pretends to be your friend.

My flesh is not my flesh, my mother made me believe: not the temple of my soul but that which she produced thus which is mainly hers, and mine only on loan.

All this I learned and more. *Unlearn it*, you might say, but how, when she told me a toy is not a toy but something you will say you love, then lose. Love is not love but loss foretold. A day is not a day but doom.

We shared our fears. My pain was her pain, she said, my crimes and humiliations hers. My orthopedic shoes, failed math tests, and ear-twisting teachers hers.

She told me she could read my mind. That she could tell when I was lying just by looking in my eyes, and lying was as bad as stealing, so why even try?

This is how I was annihilated in paradise.

And this is how I learned to barely breathe. Because the less you breathe, the less you break. The less you do, the less you can do wrong.

* * *

So here we are, we who do not want to be we. Our spells were different but the same. I understand you. You understand me.

Now let this be our pledge, to be each other's magic pebbles. We have found each other on the beach. We recognize each other. We will tell each other the absolute truth.

So speak.

The lies they told us about us were not really about us.

The lies were *about them*.

Our spellcasters, afraid, said, *Be afraid*.

Our spellcasters, feeling inadequate, called us inadequate.

Our spellcasters, repulsed by their own flesh, reviled ours.

Our spellcasters, feeling unfairly judged, judged us.

Guilt-wracked, they told us, *This is all your fault*.

They did this because someone else—somewhere, someday—did it to *them*. Some of our spellcasters were spellbound too.

No matter what inspired the lies, we had the misfortune of hearing them. Unfiltered and unscreened. Back then, we thought we had good reasons for believing them.

But living our lives based on lies that, while ostensibly about us, really have nothing to do with us is like wearing glasses prescribed for others and listening nonstop to the iPods of others, which are loaded with only *their* favorite songs, which we can't stand. At what point does it dawn on us that we are staggering around with double vision, screaming to drown out music we hate, unnecessarily?

Our spellcasters told us, *It is too late for you to get smart, become beautiful, redeem yourself. Too late*.

This is a lie. I hope it is a lie.

Told by someone who meant no harm, not that this matters, as the harm was done. And sometimes told with malice, yes. To Kristy, Keisha, Cara, Rachel, Nate, Jeremy, Joel, Tim, Jenna, Alison, Shannon, Gloria, Mariah, Kafka, and the rest. To

Mom, whose fear and pain I would have given anything to quell. To L, whose braids hung past her knees, who put herself to sleep forever. And to me. To all who listened to lies and believed.

Those cords binding your hands and feet, the cage before your face, inscribed with lies.

Resist. Relinquish all belief.

The only words you see are these. The only voice you hear right now, the only voice you need to hear, is yours—back in your "time before."

For this moment, we the afflicted mourn our missing years. We mourn mistakes made, and we mourn all those who never made it home.

But now we say: *No more, no more, no more.*

All Your So-Called "Personality Flaws" Are Actually Just Clever Coping Mechanisms

The worst form of slavery is that of the slave who has lost knowledge of being a slave.

—FRIEDRICH NIETZSCHE

Spells notwithstanding, damage done, we with low self-esteem are individuals—not faceless, marching myrmidons. You and I neither walk nor talk alike. We prefer different syrup brands. Were we to meet, we might never be friends.

Yet in some ways we are identical.

We say, think, and do some of the exact same things in the exact same situations. We share a set of definitive habits and quirks *because we hate ourselves.* We might not realize that we have these habits, much less that we share them with so many others, much less that they mark us as members of the Self-Loathing League. But we could recognize each other by them if we tried.

Now I can spot these "tells" from miles away. For most of my life I just *had* them.

Even if you know you have these habits, you probably don't know *why*. You probably just hate them along with everything else you hate about yourself.

But these habits are not "bad," not flaws, in and of themselves. They're simply symptoms of self-loathing. Red flags. Coping mechanisms. Cries for help. We use them, albeit unwittingly, to navigate this crowded, seemingly punishing world. As long as you hate yourself, you will keep these habits—*need* them, even, to survive.

The most effective way to break them is not to address them only as themselves but as symptoms, offshoots, of our self-loathing. Trace them to their source, the source they share, and tackle *that*.

Imagine these habits as garden plants. Each of them looks entirely unique, with its own bizarre array of leaves, stalks, flowers, and/or fruit. Yet all these plants are growing from the same seed, buried underground: one giant, toxic seed.

Which is to say: Supplant the seed. Dig deep, destroy it, and these plants in all their poison-fruited finery will die.

Breaking these habits we share will not make us perfect. But each one we break brings us closer to our true selves and our "times before"—before our every act was shaped by shame.

I would bet my left arm that you are not nearly as bad as you believe you are. No, seriously. Left arm. Gone, if you are even half as gross or unacceptable as you insist.

Perfection is not possible. Perfection was never the point. Now, how are you and I alike?

The Twelve Most Common Personality Traits Associated with Low Self-Esteem

1. WE LIE.

The summer I turned seventeen, I took a cross-country bus tour with twenty other kids. Our first day on the bus, an adorable surfer sat beside me. I could not believe my luck. We talked awhile, then he folded his arms across his chest.

You contradict yourself, he said. I mentioned Pink Floyd. You said Pink Floyd was your favorite band. I mentioned Jethro Tull. You said THEY were. I mentioned Syd Barrett and you had no idea who he was! The founder of Pink Floyd is who! I said I smoke dope. You said you do too. I said I had some we could smoke. Then you said dope makes you break out in hives. What is it with you? he demanded. Why are you so wishy-washy?

He was too well-bred to say *You lie.* But that was what he meant.

What could I say?

That I lied to him because he was cool and cute, so I would say whatever I believed might make him like me, even just accept me, even if it wasn't true?

That I lied to him for the same reasons I lied to almost everyone: because I had no real convictions of my own, no beliefs beyond *I am bad*, because I was raised to deny, dismiss, disown all my beliefs? So now I really *do not* have a favorite band, and really neither smoke dope nor do not smoke dope. I am that pliable, that vacant, that blocked, and that blank. In which case these so-called lies are not technically lies at all. They are true *and* false, and neither true nor false.

Or could I tell him I lied to him because anything approaching truth about myself was automatically, by virtue of approaching truth about myself, repulsive? That a sodium pentothal injection might spur me to say my favorite band was neither Pink Floyd nor Jethro Tull but some other band he had not mentioned, would not mention, a band neither great nor wretched in the scheme of things but, since I admired it, rendered ridiculous? Because whatever I liked I must also somewhat hate?

I could not tell him *that* because I did not know. Not yet. No matter, anyway. He stood and strode away to find another seat, perhaps next to a girl with enough self-esteem to tell him she thought Pink Floyd sucked. In other words, the type of girl guys like. Questions like the ones he asked, I now realize, are merely tests of honesty. It matters not what your musical taste is, only that you have the self-respect to tell the truth. If I had only known that then, I might be married to a surfer.

Why lie? Every time we lie to others, we have already lied to ourselves.

As businessman Hank Rearden philosophizes in Ayn Rand's novel *Atlas Shrugged*: "People think that a liar gains a victory over his victim. What I've learned is that a lie is an act of self-abdication, because one surrenders one's reality to the person to whom one lies, making that person one's master, condemning oneself from then on to faking the sort of reality that person's view requires to be faked. . . . The man who lies to the world is the world's slave from then on."

That's why it's so hard to stop lying. Each lie is another sticky spider-strand, connecting everything to everything. Lying is no mere habit. It's a way of life. If you have lied for long enough, lies leap from your lips faster than the truth.

Let's borrow a technique from cognitive behavioral psychology. Whenever you catch yourself lying, exact a small penalty upon yourself, something slightly embarrassing and/or uncomfortable. Jump up and down. Flick your wrist with a fingernail. Enough to make you wonder next time: *Is it worth it? Because there I go again.*

Mom lied to many people, even me. She always felt she had so much to hide. And yet she warned me that not only should I never lie to her, but also I *could* never lie to her, because with one glance into my eyes she would read my mind and know.

She told me in a voice like wheels on gravel: *You're a liar and liars are worse than thieves.*

She told me I must never lie to her—but lying to others, if it gained me approval or high grades, was fine. Sometimes she supplied lies for me. *Tell Julie you cannot attend her birthday party because you must help your father paint a wall. Tell Miss Tanaka that you sewed this blouse all by yourself.*

A child who is perpetually lied to learns to lie, through imitation just as Korean babies learn to use chopsticks and speak Korean. Would it have been so terrible to tell the truth instead?

Well, yes. Because we hated ourselves, lying was our lifestyle. The truth left us too open to criticism, too out of control.

With lies, we could corral what others thought of us. Or so we thought.

But when lies are your lifestyle, truth and untruth mix, even in your own mind, spurring the Uncertainty Curse. Every lie is a lost opportunity to learn. I have lied too much in this life.

That is the truth.

2. WE APOLOGIZE.

Too often. Always. Even when we are not wrong.

You had to watch your step with my former coworker Jed.

He was always sorry. He always told you how sorry he was. He apologized while he was with you. Later he would apologize to you again.

Sorry I interrupted you. Sorry I might have had bad breath. Sorry I bored you, wore the wrong clothes, talked too little or too much. Sorry I didn't ask about your cat. Sorry I paid your way. Sorry I made you pay.

He couldn't help it. He was beaten as a child. By someone who, by the time I met Jed, had been dead for decades. Did Jed think his old tormentor would rear up out of the earth and criticize him still? It was exhausting, his constant apologies. You'd say hello. He would apologize. You'd wonder what *you* did to make *him* abject, which made *you* abject. Then you avoided him.

But who am I to argue? I apologize compulsively myself.

I spent a weekend with relatives at their cabin in the woods. They love their cabin and the woods. Tall trees, a river, deer. They asked what I wanted to do that weekend, what I most wanted to see.

And in a tiny voice, knowing it was a mere ten-minute drive over the ridge, I said, *The beach.*

Of course! they said.

We packed a picnic lunch.

And on the wild Pacific shore, my favorite place in all the world, I said, *This is so beautiful. Forgive me.*

What? They looked around, as if for hidden cameras.

I'm sorry, I said.

They chewed their sandwiches. *Sorry for what?*

I wanted to say: *Could it be any more obvious? Sorry to be so selfish, dragging you here from the forest to the sea, which you love too but less.*

Wave after perfect wave crashed, glassy green.

How could my hosts possibly understand? How could they ever comprehend why I apologized, why I *always* apologize, why sorry leaps from my lips like frogs from a pond?

Well, I could tell them this:

We who hate ourselves believe we are always wrong. We believe that our every thought, word, want, and deed is incorrect, insulting, barbarous. We so believe this that we beg forgiveness not just after every thought, word, want, and deed but during and before. We do this because we want everyone to know we know how wrong we are, how bumbling and ignorant and rude. We do this because we want them to know we know they know.

We want this *right away*, because the sooner we show we are sorry, the more mercy we might win. If we walk right in with our heads hung low, we might be punished less. If we fall to our knees and bang our foreheads on the floor before saying a word, we beat them to the punch.

When we apologize, we are not being disingenuous. We are not backhandedly blaming others or fishing for compliments. We are not faking our remorse. That is the tragic part. It feels so real to us, that nauseous jolt of dread that starts deep in the gut and surges up through shoulders, neck, and jaw. We cannot wait. We cannot hold it in. We really, truly *do* feel guilty, like small children staring saucer-eyed at the spilled milk.

We say it so reflexively that, for us, *sorry* is a placeholder, a salutation, a reflex, a tic. To paraphrase Descartes: We apologize, therefore we exist. We are so used to saying *sorry* that it is our most familiar form of human contact. With apologies we introduce ourselves. Apologies are how we display admiration, respect, jealousy, and fear. Apologies are yet another of the thousand ways in which we show what we believe is love: by going belly-up and playing dead.

We who still sting from relentless criticism and punishment exacted long ago are hyperaware of all errors we have made and all errors we *might* have made and might still make. A specific region of the brain, the anterior cingulate cortex, has been found to be involved in self-monitoring, in the detection of errors and reactions to negative feedback, becoming activated and triggering negative emotions in people and lab animals who have failed to perform tasks correctly—or who have been *led to believe* that they failed to perform tasks correctly. Researchers even have a name for this emotional response, which can be measured electrophysiologically: error-related negativity, or ERN.

Unsurprisingly, studies show that the anterior cingulate cortex is especially active in post-traumatic stress disorder

patients, survivors of child abuse, and the children of parents with mental-health problems.

Oops. Sorry.

We say *sorry* to ward off penalties we believe we deserve. We say *sorry* just as we might curl into balls, shielding our faces with our fingers, when attacked. We say *sorry* the same way lepers in medieval England announced their approach by ringing bells and intoning *Unclean*. When we say *sorry*, we mean: *Sorry I exist*. Like the Steve Martin line *Well, excuuuuse me*. Except for real.

We stand accused. Or so we think.

Which is to say this too translates to fear. *Sorry* is just another version of our mantra: *Shut up, self!* How easy *is* this etymology?

Some of us were punished relentlessly. We said *sorry* hoping to stave off the next scream or strike, the next almost-annihilation. We said *sorry* to explain ourselves to those who would not understand. We said *sorry* to subdue those who subsumed us. We said *sorry* to stall, soothe, placate, and pray. We learned to say *sorry* the hard way.

So now we say *sorry* to stifle what we really want to say. *Sorry* blocks out all other sounds. For us, *sorry* is liturgy and loyalty, *hello* and *please*, and even *I love you*. We say *sorry* compulsively for the exact same reason we say *yes yes yes* when we mean *no*. For fear of punishment. For fear of people. *For fear of ourselves.* It's autophobia again: Fear of our thoughts. Our wants. Which might be weird. Or wild. *Warning! Warning! Opinion on the loose!*

Granted, authentic, merited apologies for misdeeds large

and small, material and metaphysical, are bold spiritual acts. Expressing regret for harm done, making amends, takes courage and humility. It might not right all wrongs, but saying *sorry* when *sorry* is justified can help heal both the harmer and the harmed.

Our knee-jerk sorry-ness is almost never justified. Our pathological apologies blur the meanings of insult and offense.

We say *sorry* unaccountably, like the boy who cried wolf. This annoys everyone. It forces them to wonder what we are apologizing for, which makes them scan *their* consciences for what *they* might have done to inadvertently make *us* think they were angry or upset. They perceive our apologies as accusations, as passive-aggressive jabs: Our *Sorry, Sarah, I am being boring* sounds to Sarah like *Sarah, you are displaying insufficient interest in me; I am hurt.* Our *Sorry, Josh, for choosing this expensive restaurant* sounds to Josh like *Josh, you are clearly unhappy here. Are you poor or just cheap?*

Thus *our* apologies make *them* apologize, albeit without wanting to or knowing why, which ironically *makes* them angry and upset. We hang our heads. They reassure us, feeling dirty and coerced. Low self-esteem thereby destroys another day. Day after day.

So our apologies are ardent. Abject. Infinite. Degrading. Dunce-cap degradation is the point. For us, *sorry* does not mean *Uh-oh* but *Should I jump off the bridge or shoot myself?*

I learned early in life to scan faces and voices for signs of hurt or offense. I knew to ask, as easily as breathing: *Are you mad at me?*

Sometimes they said *No*, sometimes *What?* or *Why?* and sometimes, with a brisk air of conviction or an eager shiver, *Yes*.

So I said—

It becomes a ritual. Like so much else: slitting oneself straight down the front and slumping nude with entrails spilling out. *Spare me*. Then that vast blankness. The klieg lights. The wait. For us who hate ourselves, living is one long game of Mother May I?

How could they know, the recipients of my apologies, that I apologized to everyone? That they were not so special, albeit my begging for their mercy? Just like this, breathless and pale?

How could they know my every step was hesitant, my every word written or spoken as a test? Which I might fail. Fail. Fail, and then apologize. In doorways. On my knees.

Forgiveness is approval, but conditional. Forgiveness is whoever you think you have wronged, saying, *I declare you excused. This time. Next time I might not be so nice.*

For us who hate ourselves, forgiveness is always one-sided because anyone, by virtue of not being us, has earned the automatic status of correctness, thus the automatic right to our apologies. Thus they are our superiors, because everyone is.

Oliver Wendell Holmes called apology "only egotism wrong side out," deeming it "a very desperate habit."

Take a tip from cognitive behavioral psychology: Become aware of your urge to apologize. Each time the urge arises, do not speak. Resist. This is the hardest part, the panic-striking part. Our mea culpas are compulsive, so *not* blurting *sorry* feels like being thirsty but denied a drink.

Keep silent for ten seconds, then the next time twenty-five. *Hold* your apology. Observe the urge: feel it from front to back, the way doctors examine glands. What does this *sorry* really mean? What does it hide?

What might you say instead? Rather than say *sorry*, forgive yourself. This awful crime, your twentieth today: Was it really so awful, after all?

Renaissance-era saints prayed all night long on icy chapel floors clad in itchy hair shirts and barbed-wire belts. With knotted leather scourges, they whipped their own backs until they bled. Such practices were said to punish sins of the flesh while cleansing the soul. With each apology, we mortify ourselves as well, believing we are punishing our sins. But how ironically unholy: making even strangers into God, we cast ourselves upon their altars, displaying our bleeding backs, telling them, *Absolve or annihilate me. It is up to you: heaven or hell.*

Sorry I have made this part of the book so long. Sorry I have made this part of the book too short.

Sorry it was not funnier. Sorry it was not serious enough. Forgive its lack of references to cormorants or Vincent Price.

No, really. Please.

3. WE CANNOT CHOOSE.

I want to bring home Chinese takeout, so I am standing at the counter in a restaurant. A miniature fountain ripples gently near the register. The manager uncaps his pen.

I need only two entrées. These will be prepared, then placed into boxes, which will go side by side into a bag. See how easy that sounds?

But I am panicking. As usual, I cannot choose. The menu is printed in both English and Chinese, but for all the sense it makes to me right now, it might as well be hieroglyphics.

It lists forty-six dishes, some with tiny photographs to help. And making my task ostensibly simpler is the fact that these dishes are all Chinese. Thus I need not choose between, say, tacos and borscht.

But still, my face is hot. My throat is tight. Soft music throbs over the speakers, giving my mind yet another excuse not to concentrate. The manager looks at the clock. Oh *hell*.

Just pick.

You goddamn wimpy indecisive dumbass. *Pick!*

Self-loathing cripples our ability to choose. Thinking ourselves inferior means automatically assuming that whatever we pick will be wrong. For us, facing a choice means automatically predicting our own failure. For us, choosing means not *choosing the best* but rather *choosing the least worst*. Pondering options, we feel the hot-cold flush of anticipated disappointment—*This will suck!*—and, if our choices impact other people, punishment. My finger trailing up and down a menu or a sales rack is the finger of defeat. For us who hate ourselves, to choose is to experience precognitive regret.

Guess what! This translates back to fear! Our fear of choice is really fear of failure. Blame. Being exposed in our inferiority, of which our choices are plain proof. What? You picked sweet-and-sour squid? Good God. Well, now we know never to let *you* pick again.

Faced with a choice, some of us freeze. We stand there spaced-out, stalling, shuffling our feet, as if some miracle might spare us: a typhoon, say, or a sudden law banning all foods but beef.

Faced with a choice, some of us who hate ourselves do not stall but rush headlong into wild, random, risky situations so as not to appear scared or indecisive. This mysterious white liquid I am drinking, this stranger into whose car I have just climbed, and my new Satan tattoo are miles better than nothing and/or looking like a wimp. Yet rash behavior, breakneck choices, also start from fear—of being unhip, left out, standing still.

Whether you respond to your fears with paralysis or outrageousness, your response is a coping mechanism for living in a choice-riddled world. Now more than ever, choices lurk and beckon everywhere, with literally countless options in countless arenas just a click away. What to watch, wear, hear, eat, see, learn, read, play, write, do; whom to tell what, where, how, and when: the very "choiciness" that some hail as a sign of progress is, for we the choice-challenged, a source of deep anxiety.

Some of us have trouble choosing because, too often, others chose *for us*—or we chose whatever another ordered, trusting them more than ourselves.

Serena Williams admits that as a child she "always tried to be Venus"—her elder sister and fellow tennis superstar, Venus Williams.

"There were two Venus Williamses in our family—it was crazy," said the Wimbledon winner and four-time Olympic gold medalist. At restaurants, "my parents would make me order first, but once she ordered, I'd change my mind. It was tough for me to stop being Venus and become the person I am. . . . I still copy Venus in many ways, but it's not as bad."

Even for those who do not hate themselves, choice is a challenge. Studies show that, faced with more than six options, the human brain enters a state known as choice overload. People allowed to choose from among six varieties of candy report far more satisfaction with their choices afterward than those allowed to choose from among twelve varieties. The latter group feels more anxiety than the first group while making their selections, then more regret afterward.

Imagine feeling *that* overwhelmed by choice and then *that* regretful afterward not only in a lab experiment or a restaurant but with every gesture and every word and thought every minute of every day. *That* is life with low self-esteem. You probably don't need to "imagine" it. You probably feel it right now.

If making choices is stressful for everyone, it is more so for us.

One day when I was very small, Mom called my name from her bedroom and said, *Bring me a glass of water.*

I was thrilled. It was the first time an adult had sought my help. I toddled briskly to the kitchen, proud to be a courier, a bringer of refreshment. Standing on a chair, I seized a glass and turned the faucet on.

But wait.

She had not said how cold or hot.

She had not said how much.

One hand under the streaming tap, I stalled. Two possible scenarios flashed back and forth: In one, I handed Mom a partly empty glass. She growled, *Why so little? Were they charging by the ounce?* In the other scenario, I gave her a full glass. Hefting it, she snarled, *Trying to drown me?*

Either was equally plausible.

Thus however much water I put in the glass could equally be wrong.

An empty glass, a full one, something in between. That was asking for trouble.

My joy became doubt, which became terror.

Wrong choices, I realized then, cause suffering. They do this by being more unpleasant than correct choices: less thirst-quenching, say, or (just ask Goldilocks) too hot. Wrong choices make us suffer by incurring mockery and anger. When our wrong choices make others suffer, we suffer as well and even more: *they* suffer merely because of an action, whereas *we* suffer watching them suffer because of an action, then we suffer doubly because that action was ours.

Which is to say, wrong choices confirm what we think of ourselves and what we think others think of us: that we are bad. That we cannot be trusted with decisions, dinner, water in a glass. That letting us decide is dangerous.

Decision making demonstrates responsibility. Decision making demonstrates maturity. Decision making demonstrates identity. And we who hate ourselves have issues with all three.

As long as we can stave off making choices, we remain untested, uncharged, and at large, leaving no mark, thus safe in at least one way from ourselves. The state of non-choice is for us a state of grace, a plateau where we breathe rarefied air because nothing is asked of us.

In our desire to avoid choices, we devise dodges and ploys.

Asked to choose—or help choose—a baby's name, a type of car, an arborist, a wine, a destination—we pretend to be polite. *Oh no,* we say. *It's up to YOU.* As if we proved our love with deference. As if we *had* no preference. As if we would decide next time. As if.

What we are really doing with these pas de deux is letting others hold the bag if anything goes wrong. Whoever chooses will be held responsible for that selection and its aftermath, in perpetuity. If those results are good, hooray. If those results are bad, boohoo. If someone else selected, hey, he or she should have chosen otherwise. Hee-hee, at least it wasn't me.

We pray: *May it never be me.* Sometimes (by force, when young, while drunk) we choose, then pretend we did not. *My parents made me major in art history. You made me marry you. He tricked me into olive green.* We pretend to be helpless victims of selections others made. Meanwhile, we wait with bated breath to be found out, for someone to point straight at us and say: *You raised that Jägermeister to your lips and drank,* or *Who the hell wears tube socks with a skirt?* or *You chose this cruise! You!*

We know it well, from every pear we ever ate that should have been an apple, every road not taken, every message sent in anger or mistaken haste. We who hate ourselves know so well this yearning to turn back the hands of time: Do over. Better yet, do nothing. Ever. Anything at all.

The menu swims under my gaze. The heart-shaped clock ticks, *tick-tick*, like a cartoon time bomb on the wall. The manager has walked away.

Wait, egg foo yong. Wait, no. My ears feel iced. What could

go wrong? *I like all Chinese food. In all my life, I never had a Chinese dish I did not like. Waiting at home is someone who would happily eat anything, would happily eat sweet-and-sour pencils if I ordered them.*

I could pick anything. I could just close my eyes and point.

What if the chow fun is too soft? What if the egg foo yong is runny? They never were before, and I've eaten here for years. But. What if? *Gross.*

And I am thinking: *Someone save me. Someone burn this motherfucker down!*

I tell the manager my order, wishing I was anywhere but here, my throat almost too tight to talk. That worry like a grater to the brain.

Self-loathing renders us inactive, turns us into bugs in amber. We know that doing nothing means doing nothing wrong. Because we hate ourselves, we hate whatever we would choose. (Morgan. Maroon. Puerto Vallarta.) Then, voilà, our vacillations become something else about us we can hate.

You could never ask Mom why she had done or said any particular thing. Oh, you could ask. But she would never say. Her eyes flashed panic, then went blank as she said, *I don't know.* Ask her again, impatiently or gently, and through clenched teeth like an apprehended burglar she hissed, *I don't KNOW.*

Which was true. She did not. She hung her head and hid it in her hands and if you kept asking she sobbed, repeating *I don't know,* her shoulders shaking helplessly. And you could ask and ask and ask but she would never answer you, because she never knew. Sometimes she would walk off and lock herself in a room. And sometimes she would raise her head as if waking from sleep and say, *Look over there—a fly!* or *The parking is always awful at the airport.*

This habit has two halves: indecision and regret. They fuel each other. Each could exist independently. That would be bad enough. But we who hate ourselves get both. Start backward. Before choosing, refuse to regret. Imagine regret as a cord you have unplugged. Thenceforth, *no matter what you pick*—hot or cold, red or blue, chow mein or sautéed brains—*will be okay.* Maybe not great, but probably not lethal. Make the most of it. Find five good things (it's hot, it's colorful, it's cooked, it has no Snarol in it, and I now see cauliflower in a whole new way) about your choice, no matter what—just as you'd reassure a child who cried, *I should have brought my other doll!*

4. WE RUIN OUR OWN FUN.

How many times have you felt overjoyed—then doomed? How many of your parties, victories, and private glory moments have you punctured, thinking: *Does she hate me now? Do I look fat?* This is the habit that is hardest to explain to those who do not hate themselves. We have fun. Then we make it stop.

We believe that whatever feels at first like joy is not. Or is, but will not last. Or should not last. We feel so sure of this that we will undermine our own inklings of joy, blunting the pain we think awaits. This way we beat pain to the punch. We will not simply sit/stand/lie like suckers when the practical joke finishes, the push, the pendulum.

We will not let ourselves be caught off-guard by joy and its evil conjoined twin, irony.

Snorkeling means shark attack. Sunshine means skin cancer. Ask us out on a date and we assume that you are taunting us plain-Janes in a cruel "dogfight" contest with your friends. Hug us and we will think you want to gauge how misshapen we are under our clothes.

Who taught us to defuse our thrills, flatten our peaks? Our spellcasters.

Earlier in this book, we met Kristy, whose father punctured her joy at completing a real-life conversation in Russian by asking whether she could have had the same conversation in Dutch. Franz Kafka experienced similar emotional stifling when his youthful joy was repeatedly mocked and dismissed by his harsh father.

"It was only necessary to be happy about something or other, to be filled with the thought of it, to come home and speak of it," Kafka wrote in a letter to his father, "and the answer was an ironic sigh, a shaking of the head, a tapping on the table with a finger: 'Is that all you're so worked up about?' . . . or 'Where is that going to get you?' or 'What a song and dance about nothing!' Of course, you couldn't be expected to be enthusiastic about every childish triviality. . . . But that was not the point."

And so we learned to puncture our own happiness before our spellcasters could do it to us. Doing it ourselves hurts slightly less. It's less embarrassing for dreams to be dashed privately, in silence, than it is in public amid sneers and jibes.

And so:

Approaching my room down the poppy-colored carpet of a

softly golden hallway at a luxury hotel on a June afternoon, I tell myself: *Have a nice day.*

No, really. Take it in. Do what a normal person booked into a luxury hotel would do: have a nice day.

My room has custard-colored walls, a gleaming desk, marble-topped nightstands, and a king-size bed whose duvet is as weightless as whipped cream. Brass-legged, satin-seated armchairs flank tall windows framing hills studded with candy-colored houses and a silver bay.

Have a nice day.

Goddamn it, have one.

For us who hate ourselves, this is harder than it sounds. Sinking onto the bed, I feel a jab of panic. A small tray of Medjool dates has been placed on a nightstand by the management, as has a linen napkin rolled up in a paper cuff. *What are the chances, I wonder, that today is the day this hotel is consumed by fire? I don't see any fire escapes. In which direction must I run when the alarm goes off?*

I rise to place my overnight bag near the door so that I can seize it while fleeing, dodging the flames. I mean—*if*.

I tell myself that ordinary people do not think this way. I tell myself: *My fellow guests are filling ice buckets and snuggling into bathrobes, savoring their views.* I tell myself that all over this hotel, people are having a nice day.

We who hate ourselves find it gruelingly difficult to have fun. The very experiences that should thrill us and warm our hearts can chill us to the bone.

We cannot accept what would normally be joy because we

believe we do not deserve it. Thus whatever *looks* like joy in our lives cannot really *be* joy but rather something wicked resembling it. A joke. A trick, like in the film *Carrie* where the title character is asked to the prom by a popular boy. She gratefully accepts his invitation, only to realize on prom night that she has been the butt of a sadistic prank. A trick, a trap. As in: *Chocolate will make you fat.*

And hey, one day I went to a theater to watch Kathak dancers from India. Their costumes were the colors of sunset, sherbet, and antifreeze. The dancers reached, leaped, arched. When I returned home, Mom asked, *Was it fun?* I said, *Oh yes.* She said, *Good. Because while you were out enjoying yourself, Dad died.*

He had. The one time I let down my guard—while watching those dancers, I had told myself: *See? This is how it feels to enjoy life*—fate showed me who was boss. Lesson learned. Must be vigilant.

In a scene from one of Henning Mankell's Wallander mysteries, a villain rigs a bomb to himself that is connected to a heart monitor. He warns pursuing detectives not to upset him, because the bomb is programmed to explode—and thus kill them all—if his heart rate reaches ninety beats per minute. This is what happens to those of us who are programmed to undermine our joy: a moderate amount of fun is okay, but as soon as it rises above a certain threshold, *BOOM*—the irony bomb goes off and happiness is dead. And so we strive to keep delight at bay, under control, lest our joy trigger a bomb-blast of fear and dread.

Fun can be had by anyone, but kept (we think) only by those

who earn it. For the rest of us, fun is a punishment, because we have that much farther to fall.

Ostensibly about to have a perfect afternoon at the hotel, I think:

You forgot extra socks, you space cadet. Whatever happens, you're like duh, *always a million miles away. Are you brain-damaged? Really. Maybe you should have an MRI. Big mirror in this room. Better avoid it. You know you look horrible. Your awful hair. Why can you never pull yourself together, even for one day? Clothes. Makeup. Hair. But no. Always the hobo. The concierge downstairs was probably about to call the cops on you before you said you had a reservation here. You look like you dress in the dark. Because you do.*

Look out that window. Seagulls in the sky. Your life is going by. So is everyone else's, but they feel alive. Not like you, Miss Invisible, Miss 65 Percent.

Someone is knocking on the door. Maybe it is a manager, here to say that I don't get to stay at the hotel anymore, that I have been kicked out. But no, it is a bellman, bearing a complimentary bottle of sparkling water.

And thus my would-be perfect afternoon begins.

I take a bath.

I silently stare out the window for an hour.

I tell myself: *You will not get this time back after it is gone. It is brief but it is yours to enjoy.* I tell myself: *This hotel has lasted over a hundred years without a fire. You are no monster. You will not be moved. You will not be a laughingstock. You look okay. No bad news will arrive today. You will simply pass through this place as does everyone else, feeling your footsteps on the golden carpet and, outside, hearing the cable cars' clack clack. None of the thousand awful things you fear will happen in the next twenty-four hours. Behold. You see. You breathe. You are ensconced in luxury. What fun.*

And when the night melts into morning, when two hundred fifty thousand lamps glow softly throughout the city at dawn, when in the restaurant I say: *Thank you for these pancakes* and *How beautiful,* how difficult this is. How familiarly difficult. And so I say: *I will not suffer this way anymore.*

I say: *Have a nice day.*

No, seriously. *Starting now.*

5. WE FAKE IT.

In diaries when I was young, I always placed quotation marks around the pronoun *I.* It isn't funny anymore. We who hate ourselves tend not to feel real. Many of us enact our daily routines feeling like impostors. Some feel virtually nonexistent. By contrast, ordinary people, those with self-esteem, feel real. It is a given, they would say, a birthright. They're born, then feel real. Why don't "I"? "I" don't know. This is about not being quite alive, about existing in the world with no idea how existence is actually done.

Around people, I do and say whatever I think it will take to be liked. This is bizarre, because I am a solitary type. I should not, at some level do not, care what others think of me. Yet I go through the motions of caring obsessively what others think of me, because I was trained in this by someone who cared obsessively what others thought of her, and what they thought of me.

With people—not all, but most—I lock into autopilot, into fake-out mode, needing to be the funny one, the one to whom they say, *I like you best.*

In fake-out mode, I talk a million miles an hour, jabbering and pointing, peering into eyes and gesturing at passing landscapes like some hybrid hostess-priest-professor-jester-ringmaster-analyst-traveloguist-soulmate-savior-seer-sage-connoisseur-confessor-skald.

I hate myself when I do this, yet cannot stop.

I tell myself it is less rude than staring silently out windows until the required time has passed. Am I polite? Or just afraid to appear sullen and ungrateful? I could leave. But hey, that would be honesty.

And hey, I aim to please.

How are you doing? I ask. *Nice shirt. Ha-ha-ha, that cloud is shaped like an erection. Is your sister better? Look, a Maserati! Whoa, a baobab! Is your burger too rare? So tell me about law school! Arthritis! Berlin!*

Each time I tell myself: *Do not do it again.* Then I do it again.

It happens automatically, involuntarily, like demonic possession or insulin shock.

Preparing to see others—as I dress, as I go out—I mouth an incantation: *Do not fake it, do not fake it—*

Do not call attention to yourself with silly gestures. Do not believe that the joy of everyone in your proximity depends on you. Do not fear that one of them might be bored, in pain, or yearning for a list of famous local architects that you must volubly supply. Do not disgorge personal data to invoke an aura of mutual trust. Do not ask anyone their dearest wish or what they would like their last meal to be. Do not try too hard. Do not riff.

I riff.

I hate this. Riffing is another form of begging, this time begging everyone to *like me, like me, like me*, whether or not I like them or want to be there. *Check out that soprano. (Do you like me?) Six more miles to Devil Mountain. (Do you like me?) Who cuts your hair? (Please, please, please like me.)*

Do not riff. But you might just as well shout instructions to a drowning man.

I tell myself: *Just be yourself.*

Ha-ha.

The "me" in social situations is not flat-out acting but rather versions of me as if projected through some kind of frightening machine. It is a fractionary me, a synthetic me. It is me portraying me. It is me covering for me.

Which is to say: I lie.

I have lied about love. I have done so and afterward felt faintly ill but could not discern why. It was because self-loathing can make us too self-obsessed for love, because it really is hard to love others when you cannot love yourself. You try. You care. You try to care. You cross a room to ask how others are. You try to care, but sometimes you cannot. Hence, fake-out mode. This is a chilly illness, such as one might feel upon waking to realize that, while drunk or sleepwalking, one has joined a sadistic motorcycle gang.

The lies of us who hate ourselves clatter in our heads like mah-jongg tiles. This is the sound of not realizing that you are still waiting for your life to start. And so we scramble to appear that we know what to do.

"We are what we pretend to be," Kurt Vonnegut wrote in *Mother Night*, "so we must be careful about what we pretend to be."

Here I go talking fancifully perhaps to skirt the issue, which is that Mom never felt real and neither have I. No one ever taught me to feel real, although you could argue that this is something one need never be taught, that even animals feel real. Perhaps I felt real upon being born. Perhaps, but then—as seen in photographs a point arrived at which my eyes appeared to die.

To feel real was to disobey her and betray her.

What strange lessons in a strange academy. Now what? Just like Pinocchio, I long to turn from wood to flesh. Some say I am real now. Should I believe them?

We who hate ourselves are ashamed to admit our sense of unreality, ashamed to ask for help, because we've asked before and have believed—really believed for hours at a time—that we were real. We told ourselves we must be real because, look, we have hands and hair and what passes for friends. We laugh at jokes. We eat. We must be real. We are ashamed to be bottomless pits of need and to admit feeling unreal because to admit this means admitting we have told a lie, a huge hurtful enormous lie that will make others sad or mad. To wit: *I faked you out. I was only pretending to be real.*

Many of us who hate ourselves experience our presence in the world as what psychologists call a "false self"—that is, a constructed persona that concerns itself almost solely with public image, yet is cut off from the "true self," as the person feels hollow, unreal, or dead inside. False selves are not created consciously as deliberate attempts to fake out the public. They are not like disguises used by con artists or fugitives in order to harm others and avoid arrest.

First named and discussed by the mid-twentieth-century British pediatrician and psychoanalyst D. W. Winnicott, false selves are formed unconsciously as defense mechanisms to protect the "true self," the authentic, creative, playful, spontaneous self that has been traumatized—by abuse, neglect, deprivation, and/or enforced compliance—and in order to save itself has gone into hiding, where it remains elusive, inaccessible, or even unknown to the individual him- or herself, who goes through life feeling empty inside or dead inside and fake outside, *without knowing why.*

False selves often emerge when small children receive no "mirroring" from adult caregivers whose love and attention is inconsistent and/or conditional, given only when the child obeys and studiedly imitates the dominant caregiver in every way possible, becoming in effect a miniature version of that adult without understanding that this is happening, or why.

The false self means well. It is, after all, a survival strategy, and functions as a kind of caretaker or guard, allowing us to function with at least apparent normalcy while protecting the true self from what Winnicott called "annihilation." Thus the false self presents a "polite and mannered" if also rigid and defensive mien. Especially in intellectual types, the false self "very easily deceives," Winnicott wrote:

"The world may observe academic success of a high degree, and may find it hard to believe in the very real distress of the individual concerned, who feels 'phoney' the more he or she is successful."

In extreme cases, the individual is unaware of having both a true self and a false self. "The False Self sets up as real" and is taken by observers, *and the individuals themselves*, to be an authentic personality. Presented with "situations in which what is expected is a whole person"—such as friendship or love—it becomes apparent that "the False Self, however well set up, lacks something, and that something is the essential central element of creative originality," Winnicott observed.

Healing begins when the true self is "acknowledged as a potential and is allowed a secret life," which becomes less and less secret in time. If I come to realize that this jabbering, gesturing figure that presents itself to others while I feel dead inside is a false self, that this false self remains at the helm oversharing, talking too fast, and trying too hard to please while down there somewhere unseen and even unfelt by me is a true self, a long-lost and mysterious true self, then I can first of all forgive the fact of this false self. I did not forge a false self willingly, deceitfully, or even consciously. These things it does are not my fault. I do not want it to exist. It serves a purpose that I wish did not exist.

This false self that I present to society is useful to me—because at some level I fear that if everyone saw what I'm like on the inside while faking it on the outside, many people would dislike me. But so what? Is it my job to be adored by everyone? I am a solitary type. One of the main causes of my self-loathing was a childhood spent denying this essential fact. Living in fake-out mode just furthers that denial. Talk about unreal. This false self is a handy little coping mechanism that allows us to function in situations that otherwise we would find intolerable. Is that such a heavy price to pay, a dash of fraudulence, if—at least for a while—it helps us face the world?

But which self is writing this book?

Ever since I first became conscious of doing things, it has been a sick sort of consciousness, the strange nebulous state of being hyperconscious yet also unconscious, hypnotized, robotic, automatic, lacking agency. All my life I have been hyperaware of far too much, of everyone's opinions of me, of their possible reactions, of their feelings and desires and the risk of their despising me and the fact that this does not matter, yet it does. Meanwhile, I have been half-switched off, numb in a way, or half-asleep, on autopilot, marking time. I'm doing it right now, writing in what I think is perfect rhythm because I am terrified that if I let this rhythm drop for just a beat my words will lose your interest, you will judge me as inferior, your eyes will glaze over, and you will drift away. And then?

I will cease to exist.

Our true selves, the selves from our "times before," are waiting for us. Where to find them? In the places and activities that make us hate ourselves the least. Do you hate yourself less than usual while mountain-climbing, singing, studying, discussing lab results, visiting France? Wherever you hate yourself less is where your true self lives, where he or she feels safe to work and play.

Seek your true self the way birdwatchers scan the sky and

trees. The more you come to recognize your true self—as it smiles into a forest campfire, say, or shines while fine-tuning a car—accept him or her. Welcome, embrace, and protect your true self as you would your best pal or your child. *See, that's the deal.* Some of our true selves' traits might be uncommon or unpopular, but once we grasp that they are *ours* and *real*, we must wear them with pride and joy as if our lives depended on it, because they do. Don't hate your true self just because self-hatred is a habit. My true self craves silence, abhors cities, adores holiday décor (not holidays, but their décor), is childish by most estimations, and would rather be alone on a deserted beach than with just about anyone or doing just about anything else. It took me over forty years to realize these essential, life-defining truths.

The first step toward no longer faking it is to stop despising ourselves for faking it. Fakery is perfectly understandable, and it's something most people do, consciously or not. *Fake it till you make it,* they say, and in our case *making it* entails first locating that elusive true self. With enough encouragement, the true self will be ready to emerge. But until then, *someone* has to be at the controls, and a false self is better than no self at all.

Thus the second step toward no longer faking it is to realize that faking it will likely be our last self-loathing quirk. After the rest are unlearned and let go, when the time for the real me has finally arrived, it will be the *false* me, the last tenant in my self-esteem halfway house, who will hand over the keys to the real me.

It's not the false me's fault. She meant to help.

This is the place to start.

False self, meet true self. Hello. Hi. Acknowledge both. And like long-separated siblings bound to save each other, each has done its best.

6. WE ARE STUCK IN THE PAST.

My friend Tessa always avoided certain buildings and even entire streets in our town—devising circuitous, time-consuming detours around them—because, she said, *they bring up bad memories*. Asked to describe these memories, Tessa narrated incidents that most would dismiss as insignificant. She had once felt embarrassed during a job interview in that office building. Boys had once jeered at her from that frat house. In that bakery, a clerk had mocked her accent—one day, many years before. I told Tessa that she was making herself her own outcast, walling off parts of her own town to herself based on ever-more-distant memories. She scoffed. Those wounds were ever-fresh.

Sages advise us to live in the present moment. "Live quietly in the moment and see the beauty of all before you. The future will take care of itself," proclaimed the guru Paramahansa Yogananda. "Forget the past, for it is gone." Buddhist visionary Thich Nhat Hanh suggests beginning each meditation session— and alerting ourselves throughout each day—with the mantra "Present moment, wonderful moment."

Well, yeah. But we who hate ourselves are glued to the past, because the past is for us a place of both enchanting wonder and hypnotic horror. In the past lie our "times before," those magic days when we did not yet hate ourselves. *And* in the past lies every failure, every dumb thing we have ever done. For us, the past is fairyland and prosecution files, escape and evidence. For us, the past is loaded. The rearview mirror is irresistible.

The past consumes me. It should not. It should not consume anyone. It is gone. It is over. This is one of the few facts we know for sure in an uncertain world: *The past is gone.* We can't go back and fix or change it or relive it. We can't. Yet, even knowing this, we stare and stare and stare through that rearview mirror down that ever-receding highway.

Eckhart Tolle asserts that the past is an illusion.

"What you think of as the past is a memory trace, stored in the mind, of a former Now. . . . Past and future obviously have no reality of their own. Just as the moon has no light of its own, but can only reflect the light of the sun, so are past and future only pale reflections of the light, power and reality of the eternal present. Their reality is 'borrowed' from the Now."

Tolle warns against becoming "trapped in time," against having "the compulsion to live almost exclusively through memory and anticipation," which "creates an endless preoccupation with past and future and an unwillingness to honor and acknowledge the present moment and *allow it to be.*" The past, Tolle writes, "is an illusion," a delusion, and even a "mental disease" that cuts us off from our true selves, which exist only and forever in the Now.

While we gaze into the past, wishing it had been different, the present whizzes by unnoticed. I will eventually see this present, but only *after* it appears in the rearview mirror, after it has become the past, after it's too late to change, after it's too late to experience whatever happens as it happens.

A mental disease, for sure.

People who don't hate themselves and who gaze through the front windshield see dangers and changes as they loom, and prepare for them accordingly. But we who hate ourselves and are thus riveted to our rearview mirrors are often unprepared for what's coming down life's pike.

As we gaze into our rearview mirrors, everyone else sees a rainbow up ahead. By the time this rainbow would have appeared in our rearview mirrors, it has faded away. And so it happens again. And again.

A lifetime spent looking out the rearview mirror is a lifetime missed. A lifetime experienced only in retrospect. A lifetime of regret.

Tearing our eyes off the receding horizon might be the hardest thing we'll ever do, because the past is known. The past is proof. The past is what we use to justify our misery. But look! Another rainbow's just around the bend. Can you afford to miss it?

7. WE DEFLECT PRAISE.

She said, *You saved my day.* I said, *No way.*

He said, *You look nice in that dress.* I thought: *What does he want?*

They said, *We love your latest book.* Cringing, I thought of my previous book, the one that failed.

I cannot accept praise.

Praise is a gift. Intangible, but just as precious and as *meant* as any wrapped box or bouquet. Even the latter are hard for us who hate ourselves to accept, so sure are we that we do not deserve them. Given presents, Mom would stash them in closets or under beds for as long as possible. Forced to unwrap one, she slashed wildly at its paper, tape, or string, starting to cry. Pulling its contents free, she turned the gift around in her hands and made choking sounds.

Praise is a harder kind of present to deflect. It cannot be stashed or left wrapped. Praise is immediate and as such demands an immediate response.

But we never believe it, so what can we say?

Thanks would be obvious. But we are so appalled by praise, so bent on informing its giver of his or her ignorance, that we fall over ourselves mumbling *But no, you are mistaken,* waving our hands as if ducking gnats.

Our praisers stare in wonderment. We might as well set fire to ribboned boxes and bright bouquets as their givers watch, in shock.

Praise reaches its recipient in stages. First one hears or sees kind words. This might be a surprise. The kind words take two seconds to sink in, a sweet private absorption, like honey on toast. Then, for those who do not hate themselves, comes belief.

For us who *do* hate ourselves, the process stops at its first step. We hear. We see. Surprise! But then nothing sinks in. Those words might as well be honey on tin.

We tell ourselves we are just being honest. Modest. Realistic. Fair. Watching others accept praise we think they do not deserve, we vow to never be like them. Beaming and cavalier, they ask, *Oh, do you REALLY like my hair?* so they can hear the same praise twice. What narcissists they are!

We know: whomever praises us must be delirious. In time they will want to retract their words. Once *they see the real me.* Save them the pain. Say: *Sure, but what you do not know is that I laugh at funerals and cheated on my driving test.*

Those whose praise we deflect—often without even a *thanks*—are often irked or hurt. They do not understand that our demurrals and denials are not rude but, to us, absolutely true.

Our flaws, our (at best) mediocrity, the wages of birth, age, and random chance upon us are so obviously irrefutable to us that even tiny compliments bounce off us like Ping-Pong balls.

Having begun his illustrious career in the late 1960s, Robert Crumb is the most popular underground comic artist who ever lived. His legendary status was already well-established—in fact, a full-length biographical film about him, *Crumb,* was soon to premiere nationwide—when Crumb launched the first volume in his Self-Loathing Comics series. Its cover sports a grotesque self-portrait in which a bug-eyed, wrinkly-faced, bucktoothed Crumb stares in horror at his reflection in a mirror. *IS THAT ME?!* he asks, then answers his own question: *MY GOD! IT IS!!*

Whatever was written in those sheaves of fan letters he had received over the previous twenty-five years clearly wasn't having any effect right then.

And really, what praise could penetrate the self-loathing resolve of Lenny, the main character of Gary Shteyngart's novel *Super Sad True Love Story,* who describes himself thusly:

"A slight man with a gray, sunken battleship of a face, curious wet eyes, a giant gleaming forehead on which a dozen cavemen could have painted something nice, a sickle of a nose perched atop a tiny puckered mouth, and from the back, a growing bald spot whose shape perfectly replicates the great state of Ohio, with its capital city, Columbus, marked by a deep-brown mole. *Slight.* Slightness is my curse in every sense. A so-so body in a world where only an incredible one will do. A body at the chronological age of thirty-nine already racked with too much LDL cholesterol, too much ACTH hormone, too much of everything that dooms the heart, sunders the liver, explodes all hope."

Good luck praising *him.*

Some of our spellcasters berated us for what they said was showing off. Maybe we liked our toy guitar too much. Maybe we corrected their spelling. *Who do you think you are?* they raged. Then they told us who *they* thought we were.

Our praisers do not understand that some of us were punished for knowing our talents, punished for knowing ourselves.

Praise faintly sickens us, because we half-suspect it is the first part of practical jokes. We are on *Candid Camera,* hesitating to accept a compliment, then finally beaming *Who? Me?* At which point a screen unfurls for the lens, inscribed with all our flaws. Praise cannot be real, *must* be rigged. That bouquet is made of plutonium.

In other words, praise frightens us. We cannot bear the notion—which amounts to revolution—of accepting that it might be even just a little true. Just as most creatures avoid what scares them, we avoid praise—not just getting but also giving it. Some of us steer clear of its entire etiquette, not praising others because (we realize subconsciously) they might (obligatorily or grudgingly or jokingly, we think) return the favor, thus trigger our fear. But just as kids who are afraid of dogs can grow used to them one pat at a time, we can ease into praise by giving some. Throughout your day, find sincere ways of complimenting others—anything from favoriting a tweet to asking a stranger where he bought his tie. (And yes, now and then compliment yourself.) In this way, praise becomes a current we can feel flowing in both directions. Praise becomes a language we can learn.

Praise is a strange gift in that it is meant not to increase our wealth but instead simply to expose wealth we did not know we already have. Praise is a light suddenly revealing your attic full of ingots, with a chorus singing *Now you know.*

Say thank you! Now you know.

8. WE ARE PERFECTIONISTS.

We are the ones who go over every school assignment, every presentation, every application, every creation and interaction again and again before and afterward with fine-toothed combs, staying up nights to tweak, re-tweak, rehearse, retool, and over-compensate. We feel so deeply flawed that even the tiniest error will annihilate us.

"The least little blemish drew tears from my eyes," Mahatma Gandhi wrote, remembering his schoolboy self. "When I merited, or seemed to the teacher to merit, a rebuke, it was unbearable for me. . . . I did not so much mind the punishment, as the fact that it was considered my desert. I wept piteously."

Some of us believe that others are constantly evaluating us

critically. And some of us are our own harshest critics. Either way, we can't tolerate the prospect of failure.

Even if we aim low (because we assume that if we aim high, we cannot win), even if we hate ourselves and believe ourselves to be hugely incompetent in many ways, each of us probably cherishes a few fields—even just one—in which we believe we excel. We've all heard—and most of us have said—sentences that begin with the words "The only thing I'm good at is . . ." And it is only through excelling in these fields that we think we can gain the sparse approval and rewards without which we would virtually cease to exist.

Because these fields are so rare and few and because we think our competence in them must compensate for our otherwise near-total incompetence, we hold them immensely precious and guard them jealously. Highly sensitive in general, we are hypersensitive when it comes to these fields and our status and achievements therein—because we falsely believe that they are *all we have*. Failure in our special fields, we feel, is not merely failure but a freefall plunge toward the abyss.

The hard worker, the devoted parent or partner, the fervent student, the model citizen—everyone admires these. Yet what makes them so good at what they do? Are they authentically impassioned, genuinely skilled? Or do some of them hate themselves and what looks like passion is calculated overcompensation?

For perfectionists, "just being me" is not enough. If we do better, we just raise the bar again. If we fail to better our best, we feel that we have failed. Rising up to, but not beyond, some standard level of competence is not enough to stave off the terrifying specter of mediocrity. So we must excel, striving to beat the pants off not merely everyone else but also ourselves.

Thirty-year-old microbiologist Leo was an undergrad at a small suburban college when his classmate Regina won a prestigious scholarship to Oxford University.

"But because she didn't win the Chancellor's Medal for the top performance in her undergraduate class, Regina was livid, lamenting how inadequate she was to have finished second. In an ironic twist, the student who *did* win the Chancellor's Medal was denied entry to Oxford, yet Regina stuck tenaciously to her tenor of self-rebuke. It was as if her existence was irreparably destroyed by not having won this medal, and no words of consolation or sturdy logic could displace her self-criticism."

Leo knew enough about Regina to understand why she was reacting this way.

"For all of her young life, she had been subject to the harsh criticisms of her demanding parents. She was simply reinflicting wounds which were conditioned in those formative years."

Having set her own bar almost impossibly high, Regina gave herself scant option but to "fail." Pursuing stratospheric, perfectionistic ideals sets us up for almost certain "failure," which does not merely disappoint us but festers in our minds as proof of our inferiority, which validates further self-loathing and prevents us from savoring whatever success we *do* achieve. But this looks like ingratitude. Regina was too fixated on not winning the Chancellor's Medal to appreciate having won a full scholarship to Oxford. Her classmates who had won neither medals nor scholarships seethed with envy and resentment as Regina vented about this "humiliating failure," Leo says.

Mariel Hemingway watched her parents engage in nightly alcohol-fueled battles that ended with them hurling bottles at each other. Mariel often wiped up the blood. Subsequently she watched one elder sister go "legitimately crazy" after hard drug use and another, the supermodel Margaux Hemingway, die of an overdose. That was her family's seventh suicide. Mariel retains what she calls "a visceral memory" of her father sexually abusing both of her sisters.

The public saw Hemingway as a slender movie star with perfect skin. They saw none of her private chaos: she too considered suicide.

"The truth was that I was fighting every day to project this illusion of perfection," Hemingway confessed. "Like so many women, I battled with the demons of low self-esteem, what I think of as a potentially addictive personality, and a compulsive need to please others." For years, at the peak of her career, terrified of illness, obesity, and intimacy, "I tried to literally 'starve' my demons—running to the point of exhaustion, eating as little food as I could."

Researchers divide perfectionism into two types: adaptive perfectionism manifests as high personal standards driving an individual toward ostensible excellence, and maladaptive perfectionism manifests as obsession with mistakes and other people's opinions.

Both types evince a desperate desire for control, approval, and rewards.

And both types intermingle—most demonstrably, as studies show, when it comes to body image. Hundreds of studies link perfectionism to eating disorders. A 2013 Australian study found that, among a thousand women of all sizes between ages twenty-eight and forty, those women who desired the slimmest bodies tended to also be the most plagued with self-doubt and the most concerned about making mistakes. While a certain amount of perfectionism can be an effective motivator, the authors of this study concluded that "there comes a point at which it becomes an unhelpful and vicious cycle."

Another recent study showed that perfectionism triggers extreme behaviors that can cause serious physical, emotional, and mental problems. Examining a large group of college students, the study found that the perfectionists among them tended to overschedule activities, focus intently on caloric intake, and aim not just for good grades but to earn the highest grades in their classes. Falling short of their aims in any way led to feelings of emptiness and self-loathing.

"As perfectionists go about their day-to-day lives, they generate a lot of friction," noted the lead author of this study. "Because of their inflexibility and unrealistic expectations, they also create problems in their relationships." Perfectionism, he concluded, "is a double-edged personality trait": useful in principle, but in practice sometimes disastrous.

We who hate ourselves often hold ourselves to sky-high standards, not because we think we're superior to everyone but because we believe we're *worse* than everyone else, and the only way to fend off that familiar old specter is to outperform the whole world. In any situation—were we rich, poor, A students, C students, ugly, beautiful—we would find ways to be hard on ourselves, to demand more, to ridicule ourselves for "failure," to skewer ourselves for things done or said *or* things *not* done or said. This is just what we do.

It is perfectionism that compels us to compare ourselves to others—and to almost always come up short.

They did not ask for this, these others to whom we compare ourselves. Most of them are totally unaware that we are watching their every move in order to pit ourselves silently against them and use *them*—their looks, status, financial solvency, relationships—as weapons with which to batter ourselves. That we use their success as proof that we have failed.

Some of us were taught at an early age to compare ourselves to others—by *others* who compared themselves to others, and locked us into this endless race. Strangers sitting beside us on buses will never know how hideous, boring, or poorly dressed they make us feel.

Wendy is a forty-four-year-old fashion designer whose parents, both immigrant scientists, wanted the best for their American-born children.

"My parents were successful people whose lives were destroyed by low self-esteem," says Wendy, who keenly remembers "my parents' desire for us kids to be successful in the obvious Asian parents' way: academically." As the family's least academically motivated child, choosing art school rather than the medical and legal degrees her siblings pursued, "I discounted myself badly," Wendy says.

"I view self-esteem as our personal reaction to how we compare ourselves to others for what we think they do or have. Perhaps I have that concept all wrong. But how could you feel you were losing if you didn't think others were winning or at least holding steady when you thought you weren't? How could you think you were stupid, poor, unlucky, ugly, etc., if you didn't perceive others as smart, wealthy, lucky, and attractive and yourself as not? Isn't there no yin without yang?

"Over the years, perceiving myself as a loser, I allowed myself to get abused both socially and at work, both emotionally and financially. I provided friendship and support to people who didn't deserve it. I fell prey to believing stupid crap that other people fed me. I would ignore my own gut feelings when I knew that, if I trusted myself and acted on those feelings, others would judge me harshly," Wendy remembers.

"I spent many years being abused, broke, and depressed. It was only when I found myself giving pep talks to friends suffering from low self-esteem that I found myself examining my own. My big strategy was realizing that there was always someone worse off than myself. Very grade-school, you might say"—and a reverse form of competitiveness.

"But it worked. I compared myself to others who were perceived to be losers and to others who were perceived to be winners and realized that we are all a lot more alike than we think."

We who hate ourselves tend to think in terms of either/or. Each thing is either good or bad, less or more, smart or dumb. Somehow, we were convinced the world has just two colors: black and white.

Stefan, a twenty-nine-year-old historian, was proud to have been accepted into a PhD program halfway around the world from his home country. But on the first day of his first seminar at his new school, anxiety swamped him. Watching each of his classmates standing up to introduce themselves and discuss their academic goals, Stefan thought they all sounded a lot smarter than he was—not to mention their excellent language skills.

"My chest was heavy with trepidation. It was almost as if there was a Sisyphean boulder weighing me down while my stomach erupted in sharp, explosive bursts of nervous energy," Stefan remembers. "I tried to calm myself while I waited my turn, mentally rehearsing my introduction. The lines had to be perfect, and the words could not be incongruous with the context, because my sense of perfection was now highly elevated. I was on alert—against my flawed self, perched like a sniper, ready to mow down my weaknesses."

As each classmate spoke, Stefan felt ever more blinded by "the looming shadow of inadequacy," a shadow that had hindered his social interactions through all of his school years and made him feel like "a man enclosed."

This too we are taught, usually by the insecure, who cannot see themselves except as fun-house-mirror images of others.

But comparisons are only thoughts—and almost entirely subjective thoughts at that.

"The thought 'I have failed' is a lie. 'I am a failure' is an even greater lie," says Eckhart Tolle. "You have not failed. You can simply reinterpret what happened and say, 'I have learned something.' . . . Why believe the lies that your mind produces?"

Mom used to say my two best friends envied my drawing skills. *They'd kill to draw that well,* she said. Then again, my two best friends were super-smart. Mom always asked about not only my test scores but theirs: *THEY got a 94 and 99? Why the hell did you get a measly 86?* Drawing skills. Test scores. Competition can be healthy. Being good at things has benefits. Aspiring to improve is challenging and sometimes fun. We just need now and then to remind ourselves that no one is perfect, and to ponder what drives our desire to excel at this or that: a richer life—or desperation to meet impossible standards whose bar we will raise and raise?

Mom asked about my test scores. Ten years later, I compulsively beat my head against a tabletop because my boyfriend could read Latin, play piano, repair machines, run a business, and comprehend trigonometry, while I could not. Startled, he asked, *Is this a contest? Does one of us always have to win?*

No. One of us does not.

9. WE CAN'T SAY NO.

We say yes. Yes yes yes. It is a reflex.

Psychologists call this quality suggestibility.

As a child, I did what I was told because my parents were authoritarian, so nay-saying them made me fear that they might yell. Not that they ever asked me to do anything dangerous or perverse. They never said *Slaughter this monkey* or *Jump off the roof.* It was only ever a difference between slightly more pleasant and slightly less. But I had to say yes. I was physically capable of saying no, of forming that word with my mouth, but nothing ever came of that except sardonic laughter, penalties, and threats. *What? You don't want any boiled beef tongue? Ha-ha. Eat the fucking tongue. We are the parents,* they said, *and you are the child.*

It became clear to me that this was true—and indisputable. The difference between saying yes and no was not the difference between right and wrong but between enraging someone or not. And as we all learned long ago, it's best not to enrage them.

In a letter to his disciplinarian father, Kafka wrote: "For me as a child, everything you called out to me was positively a heavenly commandment, I never forgot it, it remained for me the most important means of forming a judgment . . . and there you failed entirely."

Again, they meant no harm. They grew up in a bygone time when children were not asked but told. Was I born nondefiant, naturally passive, genetically likely to agree? Studies show that two out of every three babies are born strong-willed. The third is born compliant. That was me.

Sometimes I see a parent pleading with a child—whimpering: *Drink your milk* or *Stop kicking Elise* or *Sweetie, darling, do Daddy a huge favor and get into the car.* And the child retorts *NO.* When I see this, I clench inside and feel a little sick. A surge of envy—then I want to scream: *Do what the grown-up says, you little brat!* Then I try not to cry. And this is one more reason I never had children, because I would never want to say such things to them.

Because such statements stick. One study explored the divergent effects on two-year-olds of immediate, short, firm reprimands of the *Do it because I goddamn say so* type and delayed, long, gentle reprimands delivered after the fact. Toddlers exposed to short, sharp, instant reprimands "transgressed significantly less often" than did toddlers exposed to long, gentle, delayed reprimands. In other words, barking at babies turns them into Goody Two-shoes who always say yes. The study also found that the toddlers exposed to short, sharp, instant reprimands displayed markedly more "negative affect"— sorrow, fear, anxiety—than did the toddlers who were scolded latterly and softly. It's a double-edged sword. Shouting short, sharp reprimands at children who are hurting kittens is (science says) the best way to make them stop. But shouting short, sharp reprimands at children simply because you are drunk, lazy, or overwhelmed might turn them into fearful zombies.

Verbal blandishments need not be accompanied by corporal punishment to leave scars. As the chess grandmaster Aron Nimzowitsch insightfully noted, "The threat is stronger than the execution." Verbal and emotional abuse can turn saying *no* into a terrifying prospect. To say yes is to surrender. And surrender sometimes feels like safety. This was the first lesson some of us ever learned:

"The conviction that parents are always right . . . is so deeply rooted in human beings because it is based on the process of internalization that takes place during the first months of life," writes the psychoanalyst and child-abuse expert Alice Miller.

I could not, did not, and stopped wanting to say no.

Yes comes in many forms. When Mom asked me to report my every thought and deed to her as she sat on the edge of my bed every night, I narrated the events of my days as you might reproduce a TV episode, voices and all, so that she could interpret, counsel, teach, tell me exactly what to do and say the next day, what was permitted and what was not.

In other words, I must confess. This too was saying yes. *We had a fire drill. Karen made fun of my shoes.* Mom asked, *Do you like any boys at school? Did you make a BM?*

To keep a secret is another way of saying no. When you cannot say no, your life is not your own. When you cannot say no, when in your heart of hearts you believe you cannot, then all your gates are open. Anything can happen to you. Anything can come and go. Not in a good way, because you cannot say no.

You think you have no choice. You are like Gulliver, staked to the ground by Lilliputians.

When you cannot say no, everyone is your parent, your authority, your deity.

When you cannot say no, you are a child to everyone, a slave, a supplicant, a stooge.

Others ask us: Will you give me the answers to the test? Will you loan me ten bucks? Will you stay late at work so I can go to the game? Will you hide this for me until the coast is clear? Will you stop being a tease and prove that you love me? Will you let me move in with you? Will you hold this, do that, buy this, sign that, go there, give me, let me?

In a sense, it is saintly to say yes. One who never says no could in some lights be hailed as kind, helpful, responsible, adventurous, he or she who is always there for others, he or she who can be counted on, he or she who is up for anything. Does it count if he or she says yes, but never by choice?

When you cannot say no, you sometimes wish you could. You feel guilty for wishing this, for picturing yourself hollering *No no NO* or swiveling your head sweetly from side to side.

These images make you feel sick, so you say yes. Again. Which makes you hate yourself.

But everything becomes performative, a ploy to please. When you cannot say no, your destiny is not your own to choose.

But who would admit this?

Who would admit: *I gave my life away when I learned to say yes yes, always yes.* Who would admit: *My life is not mine, and what have I done to get it back?* Well, clearly not enough. Who would admit: *I have pretended all along that I was capable of saying either yes or no, that it was always up to me, that every time I said yes I said yes (twice more just now, both voluntarily, I swear) because I wanted to.*

As years went by, I thought sometimes that my life was becoming mine. I really did. I formulated symbols that it was. Yet I said yes. This was the giveaway. My life was never mine. Proven by saying yes. And yes and yes. And yes yes yes yes yes yes not in a good way. Not in a sexy Molly Bloom way. Not yes meaning *yes*. Yes meaning *no*.

I say yes because I live in terror of the next disapproval, the next doom which denies my right to exist. If I say no—

But no. So I say yes.

And thus I make myself a prisoner.

A former classmate asked for my help on a project she was planning, a website for which I would be paid a small amount to write about topics that did not interest me. She asked me in an e-mail. I replied immediately: *yes*. That night she called, explaining in more detail. Now it sounded even worse: being paid *tiny* amounts for *long* write-ups on topics that meant *nothing* to me. My voice brimmed with enthusiasm. I said *yes*.

But why? I could not help myself. I could not stop. My mouth kept running and my mind was perilously blank. Why was I doing this? I wanted no involvement with this project, nor had anything to lose by saying no. I did not fear this former classmate. But I blurted *yes* as if I did. As if she was some brutal savage stomping madly, breathing fire.

My back went stiff. *It* knew. My body said no, but my mouth said *yes yes yes*.

She thanked me. I felt as if I had been run over by a train. We hung up. Then what always happens happened: I sat striving to convince myself that it was all okay, that I had done a brilliant thing, that saying yes was smart. That the new project would be fun and interesting, that I would learn a lot, that I was honored to have been asked — yay, she likes me and she needs me, plus (as we who hate ourselves say all the time) I have nothing better to do. Meanwhile, my body said: *You stupid fucking dolt.* My legs were jittering just as they always do after bad news.

But now—too late! How could I call her back? What could I say? *I changed my mind?* Or *I never meant yes?* A lie. Only a lie would work. So I called her and said:

Something has come up. Yeah, in the last ten minutes. Yeah.

Because the truth? No way. No *way.* Nor simply *Now it's no.* Because if in some paroxysm I decline, I must say why. I must confess, even if—as is fair with non-relations—my confession is a lie.

All of this means the same damned thing. We say yes when

we mean no, say yes as if hypnotized, say yes the same way North Korean tour guides say of course those shops are full of food. We cannot refuse requests for the same reason we apologize, and lie: Because we are afraid of what will happen if we refuse. Because we have no boundaries. Because we are afraid they'll never play with us again. *Because we are afraid.*

Exception to the rule: I *can* say no on *one* condition—when *no* will deny me something nice that *yes* would win. One day when I was twenty-three, someone with power offered me a job—the *very* job, for the *exact same* magazine—that I had wanted since I was sixteen. It would have meant traveling every month, meeting celebrities, and writing about style. Without a moment's hesitation, I said no.

So no means yes. And yes means no.

But we can learn to make no mean no with self-respect and compassion and diplomacy. We can learn to say *Not right now* or *Not this time* or *I'm unable to* or *I'm sorry, but no.* We need not explain further in this brave new world.

Each of us is a doorway. *Yes* is open. *No* is shut. This door presently has no lock. It simply swings open and mainly stays that way, letting whomever and whatever in and out. What if you hired a locksmith and he handed you the key?

10. WE CAN'T STAND THE SIGHT OF OURSELVES.

"I've gone through stages where I hate my body so much that I won't even wear shorts and a bra in my house," said the singer Fiona Apple, "because if I pass a mirror" wearing such a skimpy outfit, "that's the end of my day."

I know what she means. I haven't looked into a mirror in four days.

That is, except the castanet-size one in which I apply makeup every morning. It's so little that I can only see one small portion of my face at a time, thankfully. Besides that, I never look.

Yes, it is possible in our image-obsessed society to avoid looking at oneself. No, I am neither blind nor a saint who shuns worldly attachments nor an animist who believes that my mirror image is another me.

My gym has mirrored walls. My fellow members watch themselves work out, bright tattoos rippling like cartoons. But if I keep my eyes down, I see only drains and carpet and machines whose buffed-steel bars blur everything.

I walk daily for miles, past countless car windows and storefronts and other reflective surfaces without a glance. Call it a skill I've learned. Call it a sickness. Passing something shiny, I avert my eyes. I look away from polished surfaces, including sliding doors and spoons.

Our bathroom used to have a mirror but, detached during a repair, it was never replaced. My husband asked whether I wanted the mirror replaced. I said no. He just shrugged. Not because he avoids his own reflection, but because he says appearance doesn't matter if you're happy. He says I'm attractive, which I do not dispute anymore because he hates being disputed and because, who knows, it might be true. Probably not, but at least theoretically. Really, who knows?

Not that it matters anymore. *Not that it ever should.* But long ago, before it did, I was a child with bangs and small, regular features that could turn out either way. I watched my mother scowling into mirrors. Puffing out her cheeks, arching her neck to make a double chin, she punched herself in the stomach and hissed, *Fat ugly pig.*

You would not find her fat or ugly, nor a pig. She *was* plump when young. Passersby in Central Park oinked at her. *Fatty Fatty Four-by-Four.* Or so she said. Why would she lie? But all her life, she had high cheekbones and a fine straight nose and such a flair for makeup, clothes, and silver jewelry that she could have been a cover girl if, in the 1950s, cover girls were plus-size. Which they weren't. And that's the point.

She was thirty-three when a bout of ulcerative colitis made her howl with pain and caused her to shed sixty pounds. This painful catastrophic illness did what every diet she had ever tried had failed to achieve. Cortisone eventually relieved her colitis, but by then she was rail thin and had learned how not to eat. She eked out every day for the next fifty years on peppermints and Sanka. Which is how I grew up watching a thin person telling her reflection it was fat. Because while her body had changed, her self-image had not: looking into a mirror at virtual skin and bones, she still saw rolls of blubber. Psychologists have a name for this: body dysmorphia, in which the body you have is not the body you see.

Suggestibility works like this: Say anything enough and it becomes true, or as good as true. Say *fat* and *ugly* about a face, any face. Yours. Say it about your face to yourself. Your spouse. Your child to whom you also say that everything you say, and *only* everything you say, is true. Say it day after day like liturgy and, lo, your jowls stretch, shudder, and sag. The skin spanning your neck and chin becomes a swag. Keep chanting and, after a while, your witnesses—whom you love most—will never trust their eyes again. *Fat ugly* is the curse that binds them.

This is how I learned that being fat means having failed. That being fat means being ugly. That the fat-thus-ugly are unloved, unworthy, unblessed. This is how I learned that by making you fat, God proves He hates you. If He loved you, He would have given you longer eyelashes. A nicer neck.

And this is how I learned that girls stare into mirrors constantly, which as a girl I must. But I must do it more than other girls because I also learned that our family gains weight around the face. Other families do not. They gain weight in their waists or thighs, which can be camouflaged. But just our luck, a face is always on display.

I grew up glaring into mirrors and whirling around in front of them as if they might yield different results when caught off-guard. But no. Always those same small features, the same face.

At twenty, I quit eating and spent the next few years staring at mirrors while gauging my facial width with calipers.

And this is how I learned that looking into mirrors feels like the end of the world.

Finally I reached a point at which I thought I looked okay. This was a shock. I thought, *You got what you wanted. Now stop.* When I quit looking into mirrors, I was neither fat nor thin, and neither young nor old, and neither fabulous nor hideous. Smart gamblers know exactly when to fold their cards and walk away. Alcoholics in recovery walk past bars. I walk past glass.

I know more or less how I look. My features have survived my loathing like blithe little rocks. I need not see. Not now. If I start looking worse and worse, I need not know. After a life spent caroling my flaws like a town crier, I owe myself this abstention. Call it denial. Call me weak. Call me a prisoner.

"As I looked in the mirror," wrote Friedrich Nietzsche in *Thus Spake Zarathustra*, "I screamed, and my heart shuddered: for I saw not myself but the mocking, leering face of a devil."

Maybe someday I will be over this. Maybe someday I will be normal and gaze at myself and shrug. This has become an era whose perhaps most popular activity is taking pictures of oneself. For those of us who have trouble with mirrors, this feels not like welcome evidence that everyone finally feels okay about their looks but rather like the same old pressure to *look good*, not merely passable but picture-perfect, smiling-for-the-closeup fabulous. For us, the ascent of the instant self-portrait feels alien and frightening and wrong.

My beef with God is not that He gave me this face but that He gave Mom hers. They say He knows all, yet could He not love her enough to make her look like a movie star?

But then, a face is just a face. Flesh, bone, and apertures. But please put down that camera.

11. WE ASSUME THE WORST.

I have spent weeks believing that Heather is shutting me out of her life. Or already has. We are at that peculiar stage in the conclusions of relationships at which one does not know which tense to use. Are? Were? It is that stage at which someone is not totally certain and someone else is. All that remains is a difficult conversation, which may or may not ever occur.

After five years of at-least-weekly contact, Heather no longer answers my e-mails or calls. This silence was not predicated by a bad experience or fight. We spent a Sunday together two months ago. Everything seemed okay. A few more weeks of weekly contact. Then contact from Heather stopped.

I did not realize this at first. I went on e-mailing her and leaving voice mails *like an idiot*, with no response. I asked Heather to lunch. Silence. I asked again. If this were a cartoon, cue tumbleweeds.

I e-mailed her again, this time inquiring whether she was ill. Cue crickets.

Then I thought: *Hey, this is over. She has ended it. Of course!* What did I do to make her mad, *that* mad, or gross her out or whatever it was, because the only possibility is: *It was me.* I went over our final Sunday in my mind, searching for ways in which I could have inadvertently offended her. Did I forget to ask about her eczema? Did I stare blankly out the window of the restaurant? In which of fifty different manners, while eating my French toast, was I gross?

I did not think: *Maybe this has nothing to do with me. Maybe Heather has changed. Maybe she took a sudden all-consuming interest in Ecuador or archery without telling me. Maybe she joined the Coast Guard unexpectedly. Maybe she has new friends to occupy her time. Maybe she lost her mind.* Sans clues, how would I know?

Maybe she is busy with work. And/or maybe she is a heartless jerk.

This latter concept sticks in my throat like a fish bone. Alien, yet impossible to ignore. *Someone. Else. Could. Be. Rude.*

Or inconsiderate. Or wrong.

But no. No, no.

We who hate ourselves assume that whatever goes wrong in relationships is all our fault. We assume that whatever goes wrong anywhere, with anything, is our fault—all the more when other people are involved. We perceive ourselves as the last ones picked for every team, wallflowers never asked to dance. So we expect rejection. We expect exclusion, expulsion, being made to walk the plank. We aim to protect ourselves by preparing for certain doom. *Soon this will end,* we think while being hugged. *Soon they will see.*

And how sad that will be, we think. But justified. We tried to overcompensate. With everyone we meet, we fake (or so it seems) some form of worthiness. Sometimes we fool even ourselves. But still. When it comes to relationships, we who hate ourselves live on borrowed time, and all our bonds are borrowed too. Or so we think.

But this is totally in our own heads. Our never-ending dread has little bearing on the outside world. That is, unless and until it becomes a self-fulfilling prophecy. Enter enough relationships already certain you will make them fail and you will make some fail. Predict you will drive everyone away and some will be driven away. Inertia. Reticence. Shuffling with heads hung low, avoiding eye contact, always apologizing, seeking reassurance but no amount is ever enough. To others, these habits of ours are exhausting and boring. Life with us is lots of work. Loving those who hate themselves is like swimming upstream: often more trouble than it is worth.

Sure, we were shunned. Sometime, somewhere. Everyone is.

Our error is in thinking we had all those rejections coming, that all those rejections were fair. Our error lies in believing that *we* are always singled out for exile, predestined to lose, that only *we* are capable of insult and offense, that only *we* can irritate, bore, or annoy. That doom awaits us in relationships, in academia, in work, in health, that, with some weird anti-omnipotence, we bring bad news upon ourselves. Our error puts us at the automatic mercy of whomever we might come in contact with. Since all personal interactions bear the possibility of ending in rejection, we approach every connection, even every *possible* connection, already envisioning its end. Our permission to stay in these relationships is at the whim of others, never us. We have no power. *We* are not choosers.

Or so we think.

To begin a relationship with this preset belief, that it will end because of us, is to begin with a preset power imbalance. How long before the other person realizes that he or she has been handed all the power, all the rights? How long before he or she tires of total control—or abuses it?

Steve left his forestry job at thirty-two and moved cross-country to live with Bryan. This move was clearly an act of love. But Bryan remained insecure. He posted notes for Steve all over the house, even in Steve's car, and texted Steve throughout each day. Always the same four words: *Do you love me?*

From the shower or kitchen or wherever he found a note, Steve shouted *Yes.* From his car and office, Steve texted *Yes.* He found the notes endearing for the first few weeks. Then he started to dread seeing them everywhere, looming at him like accusations, as if they read not simply *Do you love me?* but *Tell me the truth, Stephen Ray Jackson! Do you really really RE-ALLY love me???*

Steve raised this issue gently with Bryan, who went silent for two days, shuffling around the house avoiding Steve. Then Bryan started posting notes again. Dashboard. Faucet. Refrigerator door. The new notes read *Don't leave me.* When Bryan and Steve were out together, Steve would often glance up in a stadium or restaurant to see tears streaming from Bryan's eyes.

This baffled Steve. He thought: *We talked about the notes—okay, now let's move on.* But no. For Bryan, loving Steve meant fearing Steve's departure. Loving Steve meant fearing Steve.

And in a coda we who hate ourselves know all too well, Steve left. Bryan had driven him away—not with any intrinsic flaws in his own character, but *with his fear of driving Steve away.*

Familiar. Too familiar. As a child, I asked my parents and best friend—obsessively, like a windup doll—*Are you mad at me?* Because they often were. The suspense—are they, aren't they?—was unbearable. And if they were, I needed to know why. Not to defend myself, but to beseech. Because at any given moment lurked the seeds of my dismissal, at their leisure, year on agonizing freefall year.

And thus our declared anti-omnipotent impotence, our predictions of doom become self-fulfilled prophecies. Our dread of rejection triggers rejection. Our fear that we will drive our loves away drives them away. Self-loathing is that powerful. It kills.

We might as well have *Dump Me* inscribed on our scalps. Such defeatist assumptions put relationships under enormous pressure, as if they—by virtue of being relationships—were not already difficult enough. Our fears reveal our lack of faith and lack of trust, as Steve saw in those notes. Lack of faith and trust smothers love.

So guess what. Heather called me. Confused, not contrite. Busy. Oblivious. *Why did you ask if I was sick?*

My options flitted through my mind: I could lie. *That was just a joke.* Apologize. *Sorry sorry sorry your silence made me clingy needy begging flailing like the freak you SURELY hate.* Or I could tell the truth. *Silence makes me assume the worst. Silence has many causes. I understand that.*

I finally settled on *I was just a bit worried, since I hadn't heard from you.*

12. WE HATE OURSELVES FOR HATING OURSELVES.

And then we just hate ourselves more.

Self-loathing is a self-fulfilling prophecy.

It is also a perpetual-motion machine.

Because our self-loathing often spurs the kind of unpleasant (but potentially useful) habits detailed in this chapter, we end up hating ourselves even more for having these habits. Self-loathing gives birth to itself and then feeds on itself, forever finding fresh new ways to manifest and make us miserable. In that sense, self-loathing is born pregnant. Because we hate ourselves (and *only* because we hate ourselves) we do annoying, unpleasant, self-hating things such as lie, apologize, fake it, and assume the worst. We may or may not be conscious of how deeply rooted these habits are, why we have them, how frequently we enact them, or how large a proportion of our personalities they comprise.

But we do know that these habits are annoying and unpleasant. We know that they can make us unappealing to be with. We know this, and we wish we could break these bad habits. So hidden within this über-habit is the yearning, the impetus to break all these other habits. But because each of these habits is a coping mechanism for self-loathing itself, they are nearly impossible to uproot and will sprout again and again as long as we keep hating ourselves.

I want to stop being that person with those quirks. I do not want to be their prisoner. I no longer want everything I say and do, those all-day-all-night words and acts that others mistake for my personality, to simply be translations of one ugly, inconvenient, and unnecessary truth. I do not want to go on thinking *these* are my real problems, any more than I would want to take an Advil for being on fire.

I don't want my self-loathing to make me repulsive to others. I don't want my self-loathing to make me aggravating, draining, self-absorbed, oblivious. I don't want my self-loathing to resemble a contagious disease, such that spending time with me is like spending time with someone who has leprosy.

Ironically, our bad habits themselves are cause for hope. Perverse as it might seem, credit is due. If these bad habits are all survival strategies, consider what this says about the strength of our survival instinct. All the effort we put into these survival strategies, misguided as it is, is effort nonetheless and vast effort at that. If the false selves enacting these bad habits are guards protecting our true selves from further harm, what valiant guards they are.

And they have fought for us.

Once we begin to redirect that force, the fire and energy poured into our bad habits and false selves into unearthing and undoing our self-loathing, we would marvel at our power. It has been in our grasp all along.

Inner strength spent self-destructively or sagely: both are inner strength.

Hate yourself less: those bad habits will wither, drift away.

We know that even without these habits, we would not be perfect. No one alive is. Freed of these habits—allowed to be someone who chooses boldly and can easily say no—I would still dislike vegetables, be terrible at math, and have asymmetrical ears. But I would be closer to medium.

And see, freed of the quirks and habits detailed in this chapter, we could differentiate between the truly bad about ourselves and the marginal or imaginary bad, the maybe-good and the *I am not capable of good*. Freed of these habits, we would have nice days now and then, love whom we love, and quickly and effortlessly order dinner. Paradise!

And even if we cannot become fully free, even if echoes of those quirks persist, even if we still sometimes apologize too fervently or try too hard or lie, we will know how and when and where these habits started, what they mean and why. We will know they are not our fault, and that they need not stay.

The light flicks on. The choir sings: *Now you know.*

CHAPTER 3

The Ten Hidden Self-Esteem Booby Traps—and How to Dismantle Them

And I say also this. I do not think the forest would be
so bright, nor the water so warm, nor love so
sweet, if there were no danger in the lakes.

—C. S. LEWIS

Your self-loathing is based on lies. It is a dream from which you can awake. It is a channel you can change. It is a state of being but it need not be yours. It might not appear to you that you are choosing to remain this way in this hour, on this day. Yet you are, *we* are, choosing to remain this way as long as we know all we know and stay.

In our journey thus far, we have come to know that we were mistaught. Misguided. Tricked. Tragically mistaken. We know where, when, how, and by whom. We know we were enchanted. Cursed. We know we are not so bad and unworthy as we thought. We are not perfect. We might be unbeautiful in body

or mind. But neither are we terrible. This is all we know, and all we need to know.

How easy it appears, having reached a certain level of awareness, to take those final few steps to self-acceptance. One simple walk. How thrilling to think: *We're almost there.*

The trouble is, those last few steps are booby-trapped.

In the corporeal world, innocent-looking landscapes in many nations are secretly lethal because armies seeded their soil with devices that, invisible from the surface, will explode at the slightest pressure. Some land mines are potent enough to shatter tanks and all their occupants. Some are designed with hidden triggers that detonate when you try to dismantle them, however carefully.

Similarly, the escape route from self-loathing is mined with psychological booby traps that could explode, crippling us as we make our final break for freedom. These booby traps are not mere quirks or coping strategies but worldviews, ways of being, products of self-loathing so deeply ingrained, so well-programmed as to transform your victory lap into a Sisyphean nightmare.

Planted back then, lurking invisibly, those booby traps await. We want to sprint, but fear: one false step and *kablam.*

How to cross this turf safely?

Bravely. Cagily. With tools. First, a booby trap map. Also a manual. What are these traps, how does each operate, and what would make it detonate?

Whichever way we look, albeit unseen to the naked eye, they lie.

But you can overpower them with this secret guide to what they are, how they work, and how to dismantle them.

Booby Trap #1: Wantorexia

Beyond the booby traps, at the edge of freedom, a stone is inscribed with the words *DO WHAT YOU WANT.*

Uh-oh.

Many of us who hate ourselves have no idea what we want. We are the ones who cannot choose. We are the ones who do not know. We are the ones who, asked for our opinions or our plans, grow distraught or gaze vaguely into space. We are the amenable ones. We are the passive ones, the pushovers. We are the ones who say *Whatever.*

Long ago, we wanted things and knew we wanted things but we were told these things were bad and/or that we did not deserve or truly want them.

This is how we lost touch with our wants and came to think we had none. This is why we are compliant and obedient, tractable and acquiescent.

This is why we do thousands of things we do not want to do, things we are told to do, things we think will please others and/or delay punishment, things we must do (middle school, dental work), and things that seem better than nothing—but we never act on wild desires, spontaneous and strong. Because we believe we have none.

I call this Wantorexia. It is not universal, not a booby trap that threatens everyone. Just some of us, the wantorexics: numb. Victims of soul murder, wrote *Soul Murder* author Leonard Shengold, "often cannot properly register what they want." Wanting was dangerous. Wants went unmet. We shut them off.

For wantorexics, life is lived on hold while marking time. How safe it seems to seek nothing, need nothing, never yearn. How easy it is to let others decide for us, to just go along without rocking the boat.

I once knew a girl who, presented with a range of objects, always quickly reached for one. Her hand would hover over that item for a millisecond, then withdraw. The girl would look around then, guilty, like a fugitive. This happened at parties, her hand reaching for canapés, then pulling back. In stores, reaching for books, groceries, clothes—returning empty to her side. I said, *Go on—you know you want it!* She would laugh. *What? No I don't.*

Years later, when I heard she had killed herself, I was not surprised.

How can we be so disconnected? How can we get up day after day yet be so nearly dead?

Wantorexia can start in infancy. J. Konrad Stettbacher asks us to imagine a hungry baby.

"It calls out, screams, but the mother reacts only with impatience." Making a "grim face," she "grabs up the child . . . its face streaming with tears." She has distractedly attempted to heat formula for the child, but the formula is too hot or too cold, the rubber nipple forced into the little mouth.

"Instead of meeting with the expected, pleasurable satisfaction of its need, the child is subjected to pain—inflicted by its mother or someone else entrusted with its care, in other words the very person from whom the child expects precisely the opposite, namely help and comfort. . . . In the future, as soon as the child senses a need, it will be gripped by fear," Stettbacher predicts.

"Pain and disappointment cause feelings of anxiety and guilt in the child. . . . As a result, the child will develop a fear of its own needs. Because experience has taught its system to expect injury, the child becomes tense as soon as it senses a need."

Better to tell myself I was not hungry anyway, this child would say.

Even if our desires survived our infancies intact, they remained at risk of attack from spellcasters who found them inconvenient, threatening, embarrassing, or alien. Some of our spellcasters might have admired the approach of eighteenth-century pedagogue (and esteemed colleague of the philosopher Immanuel Kant) F. S. Bock, who in one child-rearing manual urged parents to wait until a child "is fond of something he is playing with that amuses him. Look at him kindly, then smilingly and very calmly take it from him, with a light air; replace it immediately, without making him wait long, with another toy and pastime.

"Frequent and early repetition of this procedure" will ensure that "he is not so likely to turn out to be headstrong. . . . If he should show displeasure when an object he covets is withdrawn, should also cry and scream, then pay no heed nor seek to pacify the child by caressing him or by returning the object. Rather, continue your efforts to divert his attention to a new pastime."

You wanted to play with dolls. They gave you toy trucks. Or vice versa. You wanted to study art. They said: *No, study law.* You wanted to live here, work there, join this, do that. They said: *No! Your kind cannot.* You wanted to wear plaid. They laughed.

Wantorexia metastasizes. Once we taste the pain of having a desire—*any* desire—denied, we train ourselves bit by bit to blunt *all* desires, to dodge tasting that pain again. Better to want nothing, we think, than to *want* and *not get.*

"I went to acting school," says thirty-five-year-old optician Beth. "But it was made very clear to me very early on that the only reason a big girl like me was being allowed to stay in the program was that I possessed a gigantic amount of theatrical knowledge and was always on time.

"Professors did all the casting and, although I auditioned for every play, they never cast me. And as they rejected me again and again, they would tell me that although I was the best suited for a role or the best prepared for a role or the most talented girl who had tried out for a role, I was too big, always too big.

"After graduation, I moved across the country because I wanted to be an actress. This was my dream, the goal of my whole life. I auditioned as often as I could. I auditioned for one Shakespeare company four times and was rejected every time. Guess why. During the fourth audition, I had a panic attack. I thought: *I'm unworthy. I'm not good enough. I'm hideous.*

"After that, I dropped theater. I'm no longer interested in it."

We numbed ourselves to the hot sweet twinges of desire because it simply hurts too much to want what you truly believe you will not get, and *should* not get, because you are unworthy and life is cruel. If you want something and miraculously *get* it, punishment will come. This thing will be taken away. You will be charged with having stolen it. It will die. It will be revealed as illusory.

Bettina, whom we met earlier in this book, described herself to me as "the girl all the boys at school barked at." Like most teenagers, she wanted acceptance. She wanted to be considered attractive, interesting, worthwhile.

"One day someone asked me out. He made it very clear, asking whether I would go on a date with him. I was so excited. I said yes. Then he burst out laughing and roared, 'Are you kidding me? You actually thought I was serious?' This happened in the hall, so tons of people heard the whole thing and laughed too."

What else to tell oneself but *I never really liked him anyway?*

Which desire is more primal than the desire to survive? Which self-loathing itself, in twenty million big and tiny ways, denies?

The more we came to hate ourselves, the more we denied our desires. We might as well have severed our own feet. But we believed in this. Sometimes we made it seem a virtue.

Those who hate themselves hate what they love. Thus we denied our desires partly to protect them. We denied our desires to keep them pure and to keep them ours, *even if this meant never feeling them again.* So slight, that no-thanks shrug that is in fact a partial suicide, not passive really but a slash-and-burn renunciation.

Wantorexia is bad enough when you live with self-loathing day after day. But on the healing path, Wantorexia becomes not just a mere booby trap but a bottomless pit of nothingness dividing us from any hopes and dreams we would (sans our Wantorexia) have. How can we finally attain what we've always wanted if we have no idea what we want and no capacity to want it?

HOW TO DISMANTLE THIS BOOBY TRAP

We are afraid to want. We do not want to want. We want to not want.

It's as if we heard that signature Rolling Stones line, "You can't always get what you want," and let those seven simple words deep-freeze our hearts and stop us in our tracks.

Thus even knowing what we want, remembering what we once wanted, letting ourselves long for whatever we long for, announcing what we want, is—whether or not our wishes come true—a holy act.

Letting yourself want—again, at last, even a little—is a treasure map you give yourself.

Imagine that you have volunteered to become a Big Sister or Big Brother to a child who lives in an orphanage. You and this child have never previously met. On your first Saturday together, you bring the child to a vast department store, where you say: *Pick out anything you want and it's my treat.*

Now imagine that *you* are the child. Your first urge is to say: *I want nothing* or *You choose, I'm sure I'll be happy with whatever it is.*

But you as Big Sister won't relent. *You can't foist this off on me or anyone else. We're not leaving here until we get something you want. And don't try to second-guess what you think would please* me. *It's* your *choice and yours alone. The only wrong answer today is* I don't know.

Look around through your child eyes. Take your time. Choose something, anything. If it turns out to be disappointing, don't worry. Know why? Because we're coming back to this store tomorrow too, and every day for the rest of your life. Eveything is at your fingertips, to test, to sample, experiment. It's all yours. It always has been.

Booby Trap #2: Nonidentity

The simplest question in the world is: *Who are you?*

But for us, it's a trick question.

How can we know who we are when our spellcasters said we were never who we thought we were, that they could make us into whoever they wanted us to be, that how we looked and felt and talked was insignificant or unacceptable or wrong? How can we know who we are when we have dissolved our lives into those of others, never let ourselves be stars but always their supporting actors, walk-on parts waiting forever in the wings?

We feel like rag dolls. Robots. Ghosts.

How can we know who we are when we have tried so hard to silence ourselves, starve ourselves, slash ourselves, skin ourselves, and separate ourselves from ourselves? We do not want to be the ones we hate. But we don't know how to become anyone else. So who are we? Sometimes it seems easier not to know.

In Virginia Woolf's novel *Mrs. Dalloway*, Clarissa Dalloway "did things . . . not for themselves; but to make people think this or that. Perfect idiocy she knew . . . for no one was ever for a second taken in. Oh, if she could have had her life over again! . . . How often now this body she wore . . . this body, with all its capacities, seemed nothing—nothing at all. She had the oddest sense of being herself invisible, unseen; unknown."

Self-esteem first requires a sense of self. So some of us have neither.

We feel unreal: not just unacceptable but invisible, not just inadequate but nonexistent.

I have wished myself out of this world and underground. I have worn countless costumes and a million masks, none of which fit. My surface self has always mainly mirrored those of others whom I aped and obeyed. Nothing else felt safe. My true self, sealed in mile-deep masonry, was very nearly lost. This is how it feels to escape a cult.

In order to fully escape from low self-esteem, we who had no selves must create new identities from scratch. This sounds fun, like dressing paper dolls or baking cakes. We could pick anything. Change everything. Witness protection program. Total makeover. Escape.

If we loathed who we were before, *why is this difficult?*

Because it entails choice. Freedom. Fear. Loyalty. We are like amnesiacs who wake up in hospital beds unable to remember their own names. Their photographs appear in papers, desperately captioned: *Do you recognize this man?* If no one comes to claim them and their memories never return, they assume new identities, buying new clothes they never would have worn before, training for jobs they never would have held. *Is this the kind of comb I like? Who knows?*

So here we are, not knowing who we ever were, much less who we will be.

This booby trap is almost mathematical in its chicanery. To love, like, or accept ourselves, we must have *selves* to love, like, or accept, and if we shed our false selves, we fear having nothing left at all. Instead of joy at the prospect of *freedom*, we dread our impending *nonexistence*. Thus we flee into the comfort of familiar misery.

But even our false selves can split in two, into the Loather and the Loathed.

You know both very well. The Loather relentlessly, mercilessly devastates the Loathed, which is a frozen, beaten creature playing dead. If you met anyone resembling either of these two at work, say, or at school, you would steer clear. In real life you cannot, because (your true self having saved itself by slipping into hiding) you believe the Loather and the Loathed are you.

And how can the Loather and the Loathed be trusted to build your post–self-loathing self? How can you choose his or her character and clothes when you hate every choice you make? How can you become him or her without regretting having not become anyone else?

HOW TO DISMANTLE THIS BOOBY TRAP

When you were small and adults asked what you wanted to be when you grew up, you thought a while and shouted: *Doctor! Teacher! Astronaut!* It seemed so thrilling and so far away.

So now we ask, again.

How will your post–self-loathing self look? What will he or

she do for fun? Will he or she prefer skeet-shooting or embroidery? He or she might invest wisely. He or she might wear bondage gear.

Your post–self-loathing self is not some total stranger. He or she is you, the true you, found again. Accept that he or she was in there all along, just incommunicado. He or she is *not* what Thomas Merton called "the external mask which seems to be real" but rather what he called "the hidden, inner person who seems to us to be nothing, but who can give himself eternally to the truth in whom he subsists."

You need only not hate him or her. Deal?

Ravi, now a forty-eight-year-old radio host, reinvented himself in college. Severe acne and the taunts of his high-school classmates triggered the social anxiety and low self-esteem that kept Ravi painfully isolated during his freshman and sophomore years. Finally he summoned the courage to pursue two new interests: theater and journalism.

According to Ravi, the school newspaper and drama club "were superficial environments, and the relationships I developed in them were generally superficial, but I grew more confident. I became more socially adept. I also got attention and earned respect.

"We *are* our values and interests, and when you find a community that is amenable to those, you will find yourself valued—and find *yourself*," Ravi asserts. But how to know which communities to choose?

"Walk through the dwelling place of your past and open all the doors and cabinets, as painful as it may be for you to examine what you find. We all receive messages, verbal and nonverbal, that shape our self-perception. Match these with what you know is true," Ravi suggests.

Leafing through fashion magazines at an airport, my friend Zahra suddenly thought: *Fashion is like languages. Some styles "speak" to me and others don't.*

Zahra realized that the clothes she was wearing, and all the other clothes she owned, did not resemble the styles that "spoke" to her in these magazines. She had spent the last twenty years buying slightly updated versions of the styles she had liked long ago. Her tastes had changed without her noticing this, much less acting on it. In the airport, Zahra took notes and tore out magazine pages that "spoke" to her. After arriving home, she donated most of her old wardrobe to charity and bought new clothes reflecting the styles she had liked in the magazines.

At last, Zahra marveled in her floor-length chiffon shift and faux-fur hat when we next met, *I feel like myself.*

We might not find our post–self-loathing selves in magazines, waving to us from fashion spreads. But we can "hear" our true "languages" in books, films, pictures, nature, music, laughter: wherever real or pretend people are. Make it a game—a sacred secret game. What "speaks" to you? Names? Colors? Landscapes? Lines of dialogue? Each is a starting point. Each is a tiny light.

Booby Trap #3: Regret

Hating oneself means hating nearly everything one does. Thus doing something (anything) is *doing something wrong.*

Shouldn't have done that.

Said that.

Shouldn't have gone there/done that with him/her/them/ wearing those pants.

If only I had done/said/been/picked something/someone else, I would be less broke/depressed/ugly/lonely now.

If only—

If—

Regret is a reflex.

This booby trap is tricky because it has pictures. Replayable images of what self-loathing made us say and do. I see myself having to pee so urgently that day in seventh grade—when I was *twelve,* at which age Mozart had already composed symphonies and performed them for royalty—but dared not flee history class or raise my hand to ask Mr. Haskins for permission, because *what would happen?* Fleeing without asking, I might get caught in the hall without a pass by a hall monitor and *what?* Or Mr. Haskins, sweet mild Mr. Haskins, might say no? Those were risks I would not take. Half an hour into class I wet myself, my chair, the floor. Everyone jeered and Mr. Haskins called the janitor and I sat in my soaked chair, saying: *Sorry! I have a disease!* which in a sense was true.

And the time, at twenty, when a coworker told me: *I tend to fuck only foxy girls but I can make an exception for you,* I was fine with that, just fine.

Regret is our own wicked currency.

Even if we did nothing egregious, never hurt a fly, we hurt ourselves by hating ourselves. Which is to say, we wasted part of our lives. It all comes back to that: imagining what few years

I have left, that I wasted part of my life and cannot get it back, that I trusted such emptiness.

We amass archives of regret. We inscribe annals of regret. Ask us: *Do you remember?* Nine times out of ten we will remember something we regret. For us who hate ourselves, memory *is* regret. In our newfound awareness, you tell us our regrets were needless and exorbitant, proof more of madness than mistakes, and even our mistakes were only human and so what? You tell us to forgive ourselves, let go, look forward. You say regret pins us to the past. *Now* you tell us. *Great.*

Wait! We were penitent. We walked on hot coals. Starved. Stayed up nights. Drowned our would-have-should-haves in whatever blinded us and if that didn't work, we drowned ourselves. Now you say all that was for nothing? Unrequired?

We cannot reclaim, redo, restore those days. Do the math. Right now I am thinking: *If only I had reached this stage of understanding at sixteen!*

It's hard not to regret wasting your life when you've wasted your life.

At the Freedom Frontier, we think: *Too late. Too late. I wasted my life on self-loathing. What a fool!*

Those years I could have spent carefree. Those years I could have called my own. Ten million sunbeams, sparrows, sandwiches, and smiles I could have seen serenely without wondering: Who hates me, who is mad at me, who mocks me, who wants what? Some eighteen thousand, seven hundred days. Those years all gone, those years fled with the sun, those years I could have loved.

Because I was an idiot! No, I was tricked! Do the math and what the fuck difference does it make? How many days gone and how many left? Who knows, but see that trail behind you, rolling rolling rolling over hill and dale and disappearing into dust? Too late, I say.

Too late.

And this is how it seems, and someone tells you today is the first day of the rest of your life and you want to pummel him. Because it is.

And you think: *As soon as I stop hating myself, I will be killed in some ironic, fluky way.* Like after all this hard work, I will step into a random taxi in Reykjavik that explodes. The more I ponder a bright post–self-loathing future, the less possible—the less *allowable*—it seems. Thus since I surely *have* no future—because I *deserve* no future—I have just the past. Which I wasted hating myself. Which I regret. The brighter a putative post–self-loathing future seems, the worse my past appears, thus more regrettable.

Self-loathing taught me this.

Regret hides itself inside regret, which hides itself inside regret, which hides itself inside regret. *Kablam.*

Which makes it seem impossible to escape the twilight zone of regret because waste one day on regret and you will waste the next day regretting wasting the day before, and on and on until your epitaph reads only *I Regret.*

HOW TO DISMANTLE THIS BOOBY TRAP

Regretting wasted time, regretting regret, all the would-haves-could-haves-should-haves, all that looking back in anger *at oneself* is irresistible. Danish philosopher Søren Kierkegaard noted the seductiveness and futility of this too-human tendency:

"Marry, and you will regret it. Do not marry, and you will also regret it. Marry or do not marry, you will regret it either way. Laugh at the stupidities of the world, and you will regret it; weep over them, and you will also regret it. Laugh at the stupidities of the world or weep over them, you will regret it either way. . . . Trust a girl, and you will regret it. Do not trust her, and you will also regret it. Trust a girl or do not trust her, you will regret it either way. . . . Hang yourself, and you will regret it. Do not hang yourself, and you will also regret it. Hang yourself or do not hang yourself, you will regret it either way."

But *because* regretting "wasted" time is *so* seductive, we who hate ourselves—who thus are most susceptible—must make a mission of resisting it. The past cannot be changed, but *can* forever be assessed. Then every passing hour spent on assessment just expands the past, expanding our regrettables, and every hour spent in regret expands our wasted time. This booby trap is smart. This is its trick, built in foreverness. Logic is lost against it. We must just *resist*.

What would it take to not look back? In Greek mythology, the musician Orpheus—devastated by the death of his beloved bride Eurydice—plays such beautiful mourning music that Hades and Persephone, rulers of the Underworld, make a deal with him. Orpheus is permitted to enter Hades and bring Eurydice back to the world of the living, with one condition: throughout their entire journey back to Life, Orpheus must walk in front of Eurydice and never look back. Even one backward glance, he is warned, will plunge Eurydice back to Hades forever.

The New Testament includes a similar story: that of Lot and his family, whom angels urged to flee the city of Sodom: "Escape for thy life; look not behind thee, neither stay thou in all the plain; escape to the mountain, lest thou be consumed," an angel told Lot. As God "rained upon Sodom . . . brimstone and fire," the family rushed toward the nearby town of Zoar. Lot led the way, following the angel's decree: "But his wife looked back from behind him, and she became a pillar of salt."

Resist looking back in regret *as if your current and future life and the current and future lives of your dearest ones depended on it.* Because it does. They do. Like all bad habits, this one can be broken. It might take prayer. It might take conditioning techniques. (As soon as you catch yourself regretting, *firmly turn your attention to something else*, something positive: a song, pictures of your "happy place," whatever you would like to learn, real or imaginary tennis games.)

It all boils down to harm. Have your actions caused harm? Most things we regret caused no harm. They drifted harmless into history, no worse or better than ten billion random acts. Most *things* we regret caused no harm. Regret itself caused harm. This too we must accept: this tendency, this pair of useless claws we wear that reach forever backward, slashing at thin air. *Oh there they go again!*

If you have done no harm, accept this fact and stop regretting. If you have done harm, accept responsibility. Yes, we who hate ourselves are capable of harm. Charged with embezzling more than $300,000 from the company where she worked as a secretary, Kylie Thompson claimed that she took the money because sexual harassment on the job had made her "feel worthless." Having bought first-class flights, French champagne, helicopter joyrides, and other luxuries aimed at raising her self-esteem, Thompson was jailed in 2012 after vowing to repay the full amount. Asked about his history of violence toward women, ex-boxer Mike Tyson expressed his self-loathing and his regrets in a 2013 interview: "I was violent towards everybody. . . . I hated myself and I wanted them to feel the pain that I felt."

But we who hate ourselves usually harm only ourselves. At dozens of blogs whose titles include the phrase *I hate myself*, I read the anguished writings of eloquent, intelligent, warm-hearted people, most of whom write longingly of suicide. Attractive men and women, boys and girls, post pictures of themselves, ostensibly to show their unlivable ugliness. Five years, ten years, twenty-five years hence, if these tortured souls have let themselves survive, will they revisit their blogs, remember those days and nights they won't get back, and wonder: *WTF?*

We want to rail at ourselves, *Stupid stupid stupid girl* or *Stupid stupid stupid boy,* but we must not, and that's the deal.

In order to release regret, we must make amends to ourselves.

Amends-making plays a key role in the 12 Steps of Alcoholics Anonymous. Step 8 is completed when we have "made a list of all persons we had harmed, and became willing to make amends to them all." Step 9 is completed when we have "made direct amends to such people wherever possible, except when to do so would injure them or others." Amends are not mere apologies, but rather the process of restoring justice in as concrete a manner as possible so that it is an effective action rather than just a feel-good gesture.

For instance, say you now regret (and want to make amends for) the fact that you spent many years hating your body. You can't undo the insults. Nor is a spa visit or saying *I'm beautiful!* likely to have any lasting effects. But learning to cook healthy foods or adopting a fun physical hobby are effective amends. Just living differently is a form of amends. Relishing the present moment is amends. Resisting regret is amends.

After Step 9, the "Big Book" of Alcoholics Anonymous promises:

"If we are painstaking about this phase of our development, we will be amazed. . . . We are going to know a new freedom and a new happiness. We will not regret the past nor wish to shut the door on it. We will comprehend the word serenity and we will know peace. No matter how far down the scale we have gone, we will see how our experience can benefit others. That feeling of uselessness and self-pity will disappear. We will lose interest in selfish things and gain interest in our fellows. Self-seeking will slip away. Our whole attitude and outlook upon life will change. Fear of people and of economic insecurity will leave us. We will intuitively know how to handle situations which used to baffle us."

Amends made, forgiven, move on. Because today. Is the first day.

Right here and right now, we must simply say okay.

Face forward and walk on.

This is the bravest act.

Booby Trap #4: Fear

If I love you, I will picture you being swept away by a huge wave, screaming as you drown. If I love you, I will imagine you driving off cliffs, getting your hair caught in a power saw, having your throat slit by a psychopath, or simply—probably while laughing, at a party—dropping dead.

If I let my mind wander, it will wander into hospital rooms where you and I lie mangled, burned, bomb-blasted, riven with disease. One day when I was thirty, an aunt I barely knew told me: *You refuse to have babies because you're selfish.* No. The reason I am childless is that I did not want to ruin those ostensible children's lives by rushing them to doctors daily, thinking every cut and cough signified cancer and flesh-eating viruses. I did not want to terrify them into thinking they were ill or terrify them with the fact that they terrified me. I did not want to terrify them with my terror, so I saved them by not having them.

Just as we regret regret, we also fear fear.

We the fear-driven live in fear because we were frightened back then. Not fleetingly, by scary masks or spiders or big brothers who abashedly apologized, but lastingly and deeply, maybe many, many times, by things and people we could not escape. We came to fear every possible circumstance in which our weakness, ugliness, inadequacy, immaturity, falsity, and/or general fucked-up-edness might be on display. Hence, autophobia.

The more afraid we were, the more helpless we felt, then hated ourselves for our impotence. We devised safety measures to wall off our endless fear. Most of these measures made us numb. What are addictions if not anesthetics, anyway?

We the fear-driven, we the autophobic, do not wake each morning wondering: *What will I do today?* but wake to wonder: *Today, will I die?*

Whether or not we have been tagged with post-traumatic stress disorder, phobias, social anxiety, or other fear-based diagnoses, we the fear-driven shiver frozen in emotional paralysis. They say freedom awaits. Freedom from spells and curses. Freedom from the past. Freedom from vicious voices in our heads.

Uh-oh.

For us the fear-driven, freedom is endless possibility, which is a problem because, to us, possibility translates to *What? Could?? Possibly??? Go???? Wrong?????*

For us the fear-driven, freedom is endless opportunity, which is a problem because, to us, opportunity means opportunity to fail.

For us the fear-driven, freedom is change.

For us the fear-driven, change goes in only one direction.

For us the fear-driven, freedom is freefall.

We have been there before. We know the cold whoosh of midair.

"My Mother Dear," wrote the seventeenth-century philosopher Thomas Hobbes, "did bring forth Twins at once, both me and Fear."

When I was eighteen and preparing to leave home for college, Mom told me that henceforth, in any questionable situation that mandated a decision on my part, I must imagine her face and Dad's face floating side by side in the air. *How would our faces look,* she asked, *if you did this or that?* And by this method I could gauge every potential choice: the expressions on their imaginary faces floating in midair like cartoon moons. But hey, it worked.

I moved to Berkeley, half a state away. The first people I met—a skinny man who shouted poems on a bus, a fat wine-guzzling oaf who said his name was Doctor Love, a girl who tried to steal my shoes—were visibly insane. This was a foreign place, weather and all. It was also a famous place, a legend, but chilly and cracked. My roommate in a flat whose carpet hopped with fleas poured Diet Pepsi over Special K, which she chewed loudly in the dark of night while perched on her bed, facing mine.

One autumn day, my head hurt. For the first time in my life, the first time of which would be hundreds over the next thirty years, I became instantly convinced that this was terminal, a brain tumor, a hemorrhage, a stroke. I hurried to the campus hospital, where I was reassured. Two weeks later, I broke out in a rash. Back to the hospital. They told me it was stress-related. Two weeks later, back again, telling a nurse I could not breathe.

At school, I scored A-minuses. I could not drop out. I could not run back home to Mom and Dad and sunshine. No. This was a grown-up school with a grown-up history in a grown-up town in which even the crows and ambulances screamed: *Grow up, grow up, grow up.*

I learned a trick that stanched some of my fears. I thought I had invented it. I did not know my trick already had a name, bulimarexia. I could not run back home to Mom and Dad but I could call home three times a day. Dialing felt like delivery.

Mom asked, *Are you sick? Pregnant? Fat?*

Between calls, I imagined their floating faces. Should I study or sleep? Should I drink wine with Doctor Love?

Even then, I thought I was free. In my black beaded sweater, I looked free.

I was afraid.

And no, I never was assaulted. Never was washed overboard or chased by wolves or lost a leg or saw dear comrades engulfed by an avalanche. You see, fear need not start with butchery. It can be little things.

And in the shady lanes of Berkeley, when I looked inside myself for nerve or comfort or instruction I found nothing, just a sheer cold hardness slippery to touch and a metallic swirling sound as you might find in bottomless but empty wells, that echo roaring only *no no no* but not in what you could call even a remotely human voice, and down and down and one night, sitting on a street corner, a boy said to me: *Why don't you just let me love you?* which he really meant to do, and I heard only *no no no* and saw reflections racing past and it was freefall. It was always freefall and sometimes, on bad days, it still is.

Mom used to wish I would marry a doctor. I wished for this too. Mom thought: *Doctors make money.* I thought: *I could show my doctor-husband every ersatz symptom I perceived, even at 3 a.m., and he could console me or cure me every time.*

I was so fearful that I did not see my fear as such. I thought the way I felt was called *grown-up.* And grown-ups navigated a wide world of fault, calamity, and snapping jaws. Children hide from the terrifying world; grown-ups break trails. *Of course* it remains terrifying. I did not yet realize that the terror resided solely in me.

Fear is so much of me that the idea of losing my fear feels like amputation. If I am Miss 65 Percent, and even this marginal fraction of a human being comprises mostly fear connecting strands of this and that, and I shed fear, which is all I have ever known, *what will be left?* I ask myself without asking myself, without wanting to know.

And yes, fear is a form of self-absorption. Ensconced in our safety measures, we cannot be touched. As I could not. And year after year, rain or shine, stayed afraid.

Fear is processed in the brain by an almond-shaped structure called the amygdala. Researchers have argued for decades about the exact neurocircuitry involved. A woman with a rare genetic disorder, Urbach-Wiethe disease, which destroyed her amygdala in childhood, startled scientists—as detailed in a 2010 study—with her apparent lack of fear. Patient SM, as she is known to science, laughed in haunted houses, calmly reached for tarantulas and poisonous snakes, watched horror films happily, and felt no fear even while being held up at gunpoint and knifepoint, more than once. Patient SM is otherwise normal emotionally. We are not supposed to envy Patient SM, because fear serves an evolutionary purpose, alerts us to danger, might save our lives, triggers fight or flight. We are not supposed to envy Patient SM, but it is tempting.

What if you won the lottery? What if your life stretched out to the horizon, all yours to design? This is freedom. It frightens us.

Lottery winners sometimes keep their dreary day jobs because the idea of infinite free time and fortune terrifies them: all that open-endedness.

We the fear-driven are not only not like Patient SM, but also not like even ordinary people who face ordinary challenges *or ordinary people who face ordinary happy days* without having panic attacks.

We are afraid of food. We are afraid of fun. We are afraid of dogs and lakes and death. We are afraid of ourselves: autophobia.

We are afraid of life.

HOW TO DISMANTLE THIS BOOBY TRAP

"I was a coward," Mahatma Gandhi confessed. "I used to be haunted by the fear of thieves, ghosts, and serpents. I did not dare to stir out of doors at night. Darkness was a terror to me. It was almost impossible for me to sleep . . . without a light in the room."

Life is full of danger. On this point, we the fear-driven are correct and more honest than most.

We are prepared for what *could* happen, but a little *too* prepared.

What would you say to someone who brought *two* umbrellas outside on a rainy day?

Some of the finest minds since time began have sought solutions to anxiety. Among other tools, they devised cognitive behavioral therapy. Exposure therapy. Pharmaceuticals. Faith.

And meditation, which can teach us to reduce the speed and intensity of our reactions to fear-triggers as it teaches us to calmly observe our passing thoughts, without involvement—letting them drift past our deep, still consciousness like floating leaves. Over time—even after just thirty minutes daily for two months, as recent studies show—a formerly fearful mind can "take on a positive shape" for the long term, according to neuropsychologist and *Buddha's Brain* author Rick Hanson.

Being afraid of fear keeps fear in dark corners of our subconscious and unconscious, where it grows. Shining the bright light of consciousness on our fears can shrink them, according to many new studies, including one in which four groups of arachnophobes—people terrified of spiders—were seated near a live tarantula. The first group was instructed to describe the authentic emotions aroused in them by the tarantula, saying things such as: *That big ugly bug scares me to death.* The second group was instructed to discuss the tarantula in neutral terms *not* conveying fear, such as: *I'm not afraid of that little thing.* The third group was instructed to say things totally irrelevant to the spider, such as: *Salem is the capital of Oregon.* The fourth group was instructed to say nothing.

All four groups were then asked to approach a tarantula as closely as possible. The researchers measured how close each participant could get to the spider. They also gauged physiological stress signals such as perspiration.

The first group, whose members had been encouraged to discuss their fears honestly, was able to get far nearer to the spider than the other three, and sweated much less. In fact, the participants who did best of all in this experiment were those members of the first group who had used the largest number of negative words when voicing their fears.

This intrigued the researchers, who noted that the instructions given to the *second* group—to claim they *weren't* afraid of something that scared them—"is the usual approach for helping individuals to confront the things they fear." But *it didn't work*. The more honest participants were allowed to be, the less they had to pretend not to be afraid, the more courageous they actually became. Fearful people do better, the lead researcher added, when they can freely "verbalize their feelings . . . and say, 'I feel scared and I'm here.' They're not trying to push it away and say it's not so bad. Be in the moment and allow yourself to experience whatever you're experiencing," she said.

Voicing our fears is ironically brave, because in so doing we overcome another fear: that of being mocked or shamed for cowardice. Granted, voicing *all* our fears *all* the time would make us unbearable company, even to ourselves. But voicing our fears to a reasonable degree is an act of self-acceptance that can strengthen us and reveal to us that we are not alone.

And who can teach us how to voice our fears to a reasonable degree? The Cowardly Lion, of course.

In *The Wonderful Wizard of Oz*, he snaps at Dorothy's little dog, Toto. Dorothy slaps him and says, "You are nothing but a big coward."

"I know it," the Lion laments, hanging his big head in shame. "I've always known it. . . . I suppose I was born that way. All the other animals in the forest naturally expect me to be brave, for the Lion is everywhere thought to be the King of Beasts. . . . It is my great sorrow, and makes my life very unhappy. But whenever there is danger, my heart begins to beat fast. . . . My life is simply unbearable without a bit of courage."

The Scarecrow helpfully points out that at least the Lion has a brain. The Tin Woodsman helpfully points out that at least the Lion has a heart. Dorothy helpfully welcomes him into their group. As they cross the Land of Oz (a "strange and beautiful country" which is booby-trapped with winged monkeys, soporific poppies, tiger-headed monsters called Kalidahs, and a wicked witch), the Lion finds himself drawing upon his strengths to help his friends and ensure their arrival in the Emerald City (where they hope to gain a heart, a brain, courage, and a passage home). He leaps again and again over a deep chasm in order to carry each of them across. When the group is cornered by Kalidahs, the Lion bravely tells Dorothy, "We are lost, for they will surely tear us to pieces with their sharp claws. But stand close behind me, and I will fight them as long as I am alive."

Having survived, they finally reach the Emerald City, where the Lion begs the Wizard for courage. You already have it, the Wizard tells him: "You have plenty of courage, I am sure. . . . All you need is confidence in yourself. There is no living thing that is not afraid when it faces danger. The true courage is in facing danger when you are afraid, and that kind of courage you have in plenty."

You have carried others on your back across deep chasms. You have fought monsters and survived. You know you have.

Booby Trap #5: Silence

Having come this far, we face a stark dilemma. Under what circumstances should we speak aloud about our years spent with low self-esteem? Should we mention them to new acquaintances? At family gatherings? Job interviews? Raucous parties? *I can eat cake now, sure thing, but not in my old anorexic days because I used to hate myself.*

Everyone talks about themselves, their histories. It's natural. It's how our species builds relationships: *I trust you enough to say: Here's my past. What's yours?*

My memory is my own personal Library of Alexandria, the only remaining archive of my life. If I burn myself down and cerate a new self, an entire civilization will have been lost. Yes, a twisted civilization of pain and suffering and lies, but a civilization nonetheless, with its own unique culture and rituals. I cannot destroy it so cavalierly. So I sit alone in the echoing hallways, obsessively reading and rereading parchment scrolls that document past atrocities. I must preserve them. I must. There is no one left but me.

Shame, regret, and belief that our self-loathing is deserved conspire to isolate and muzzle us. Breaking the silence marks a milestone on the healing path. We have as much right as anyone else to talk about our past pain, but how much? And when?

We are stuck with our stories. In the rigorous realm of real life, as others speak of turbines, hedge funds, Chardonnay, and Bangalore, should we talk about sorrow, madness, loyalty, and lies?

If so, who could blame anyone for shunning us?

Such self-obsessed sob stories never segue gently into the pitter-patter of car pool or cocktail conversations. They are too unrelatable, too depressing, too strange. We wish these weren't our stories and that self-loathing wasn't our history, but they are and it is. Facing the post–self-loathing world, we are ashamed, angry, afraid, and insecure about admitting that we spent so long ashamed, angry, afraid, and insecure. Once we no longer loathe ourselves, will speaking of self-loathing moor us in self-loathing not as an identity but as a tapestry, a repertoire, a theme? How much or little can we talk about self-loathing in our post–self-loathing lives and still feel free? We don't want to be scary psychos like the Ancient Mariner in Coleridge's poem, who ranted at strangers about "the Nightmare LIFE-IN-DEATH," which terrorized him after he slew an albatross. Speaking of self-loathing can feel sad, infuriating, dull—like describing life in a barren cell. Not speaking of self-loathing can feel like pretending that we have no past.

Sip. *I picked up my doctorate at Yale and rowed solo around the world before clerking at the Supreme Court and then deciding to leverage my quantum computing background into a cool billion.* Sip. *And what have YOU been doing these last twenty years?* Gulp. *Uh, pretty much sitting alone in the dark, avoiding mirrors.*

I am a solitary type, but most are not. Meeting new people always makes me wonder: *mention my low self-esteem—in* passing, *in relation to topics at hand, as history, as context, as humor—or not?* How relevant is it to anything? Well, totally. Yet also not. We don't want every post–self-loathing conversation to resemble a confessional when we have no sins to confess.

I meet old friends. Inevitably, we trade memories. *Remember when we saw the luna moth? Remember Ted in seventh grade who was obsessed with James K. Polk?* We were in the same places at the same times but with one big difference between us. We reenter those past scenes on parallel tracks. They see the moth again, and Ted. *I* see the moth and Ted again and flinch again, sick again with whatever dread I felt on that night and that day, whatever is-she-mad-at-me, whatever I-look-fat-in-this, whatever uh-oh, this-is-fun, whatever certainty that something would go wrong and it would be my fault. *They* look back and see experiences. *I* look back and want to rescue my small self *and* lie under a steamroller at the same time. When we were young, we did not speak of my self-loathing. I was not aware of it as such. I simply thought it was the only way to feel.

But now I know. This knowledge separates me from my friends. I spent our years together desperately begging them for reassurance, doing whatever I thought they wanted, bribing them with gifts and bursting into tears for fear that they were furious at me. They felt and did no such things toward me. *Their* mommies did not tell them *You're fat, you have brown teeth, your friends are bitches, and if you ride a bike, you might fall off and die.* Looking at us, you would have just seen little girls. You wouldn't know. Speaking with old friends about the present and past, I find myself now (but never before) speaking as One Who Knows, saying *I stayed up all that night regretting what I said to you in Spanish class* and *Well, I always thought you hated me because Mom said you did.*

They give me shocked, quizzical looks, saying: *You still remember stuff from seventh grade?* Well, yeah. I not only remember them, *they feel like yesterday.* My rear-view mirror is that clear. Then I think: *Shut up. It's the past. Who cares?*

Self-loathing has given us anthems, ingrained in our hearts and throats. Who except us knows these lyrics and tunes?

Self loathing has given us archives, huge annals of history, humiliating codexes, timelines incised in stone. Who except us has memorized these names and dates?

HOW TO DISMANTLE THIS BOOBY TRAP

In Akron, Ohio, in 1935, a surgeon and a stockbroker met and realized that they both had the same problem: alcoholism. Talking with each other about their addiction proved therapeutic; together, they founded Alcoholics Anonymous, whose meetings allowed sobriety-seeking alcoholics to share their stories in an atmosphere of friendship, support, and safety. A revolutionary concept when AA began, the support-group model has since saved countless lives. *Talking helps.*

And no, you're not alone.

You are one among millions.

Self-loathing is traumatic. Although post-traumatic stress disorder is well-known, psychiatrist Judith Herman expanded it to introduce the concept of *complex* post-traumatic stress disorder, which can afflict survivors of long-term, chronic trauma—such as prison-camp and sexual-trafficking survivors and survivors of years-long child abuse or domestic violence. CPTSD symptoms—all too familiar to us who hate ourselves— include shame, guilt, self-loathing, sorrow, numbness, explosive anger, idealization of the perpetrator, a sense of detachment, a sense of not being in the body, a sense of not being real, a sense of isolation, and a sense of being totally different from all other human beings.

Recovery from trauma is a multipronged process. First, survivors must be made to feel safe. Next, they must do what psychologists call "reconstructing the trauma": that is, freely *talking* about the traumatic events.

"Reconstructing the trauma," Herman explains, "is ambitious work" that requires the survivor to travel "back and forth in time from her protected anchorage in the present to immersion in the past," where traumas can be assessed and understood with full knowledge that they cannot annihilate us now. At some point in the process, survivors ask why whatever happened to them happened. This bold undertaking, Herman explains, "challenges an ordinary person to become a theologian, a philosopher, and a jurist."

Deciding where and when to break the silence is a judgment call. We don't want to be wet blankets, but how to start the dialogue? How to make self-loathing no longer something we're too ashamed to talk about, when talking might help others or ourselves? Be the first on your block to start a self-loathing support group. Call it SLAG: Self-Loathing All Gone. Or SLOB: Self-Loathing Oblivion-Bound. *Hello! My name is Tyler and I hate myself.*

Self-loathing happened to you. It is not your fault, but it is still your history. It need not be your jail. Speak up. Speak out. So what if not everyone understands? Some will.

And some will understand so well that they will thank you. Some have been beside you all along.

Whether you ever saw or heard them, they were there. *We* were.

Booby Trap #6: Immaturity

Self-loathing stunts our growth. And arrested development is embarrassing. Now hand over that sippy cup.

Whatever made us hate ourselves was traumatic. As traumas usually do, those events trapped us in their time and place. We might inhabit adult bodies, we might appear to function in the present moment, might appear to have moved on or never to have endured traumas to begin with, but self-loathing keeps us stuck. Try as we might to make up for lost time, we remain to some extent, through no fault of our own, frozen at whatever age we were when we started hating ourselves. We are *retarded*, not in the slang sense but literally, actually.

Our spellcasters said: *Stand in that corner thinking about what you did wrong until I say you can come out.* They never said we could come out. So still we stand. We are the left-behind.

What fight, what fright, what sight somewhere back there told you to stop, stop, *stop* and though part of you moved on, part of you, some still-sore part, could not?

Trying to act grown up becomes another way of faking it. Seeing "myself" "working" in "offices," "dressed up," obeying "my boss," completing "my shift," "commuting" during "rush hour" to "my house" and "cooking dinner" felt, for decades, like seeing a dull but desperately determined stranger. We are the ones at whom is shouted: *Grow the hell up!*

We wish. But we tremble at thresholds, seeing them not as bright gateways wreathed in welcome but as made of skulls and bones, their stepping-stones actually trapdoors. How could anyone as infantile as we are enter Grown-up World? It is a task for navigators, soldiers, saviors, not dumb thumb suckers like us.

Living in fear that our puerility will be revealed, we strive to hide it. But like babies waving wineglasses and wearing high-heeled shoes, we just make adults laugh.

And it's like being held back a year in school: everyone can see that the held-back child is bigger and older than everyone else in that grade, so everyone assumes the held-back child is dumb.

What if you were held back not one year but twenty-five? Or forty? Not in school but in life? What if in some ways you are essentially a toddler?

Here is what I would be ashamed for you to know about me:

I assume that anyone wearing a wristwach is older than I, that he or she is a busy professional who needs to know what time it is. Watching teenagers amble down the street, I think: *Uh-oh! The big kids!*

If I knew that I could get away with it, I would sit in the middle of my living room all day playing with toys.

So now you know.

HOW TO DISMANTLE THIS BOOBY TRAP

With healing comes maturity. But we the immature, because we are still immature, have little patience and can't wait. This is the booby trap that gives us the finger, sticks out its tongue at us, and taunts *Haaaa-ha*.

We can outwit it by waiting it out. Which is best done when we are looking elsewhere. Maturity slows to a crawl and sometimes stops while it is being watched. Don't focus on it. Trick it by turning your back and theatrically tiptoeing away.

Meanwhile, everything else you do and have been doing to stem your self-loathing makes you grow. This occurs incrementally, with every lesson learned and every flash of understanding, every habit wrestled to the ground. We cannot *see* wisdom increasing, awareness intensifying, courage rising—but they *are.*

Because of where we've been, we might not ever *totally* grow up. Is that so bad? Other adults spend fortunes trying to revive their inner children, trying to be wide-eyed, curious, creative, playful, even vulnerable again. We are already that way. We have always been that way, and we can stay that way. Bring hard-won wisdom, courage, and awareness into it, but candor, laughter, tender sympathy for crying kings and birds with broken wings: these we can keep.

The Chronicles of Narnia author C. S. Lewis, who was also a noted theologian, understood this.

"To be concerned about being grown up, to admire the grown up because it is grown up, to blush at the suspicion of being childish; these things are the marks of childhood and adolescence," Lewis wrote in 1966. "Young things ought to want to grow. But to carry on into middle life or even into early manhood this concern about being adult is a mark of really arrested development. When I was ten, I read fairy tales in secret and would have been ashamed if I had been found doing so. Now that I am fifty I read them openly. When I became a man I put away childish things, including the fear of childishness and the desire to be very grown up."

Those who don't understand "accuse us of arrested development because we have not lost a taste we had in childhood. But surely arrested development consists not in refusing to lose old things but in failing to add new things? I now like hock"— a type of wine—"which I am sure I should not have liked as a child," Lewis wrote. "But I still like lemon-squash. I call this growth or development because I have been enriched."

Enrichment continues apace.

Dismantling all the *other* booby traps dismantles this one. Now we say: *Haaa-ha.*

Booby Trap #7: Quitterism

It's hard to succeed at anything when you always quit before you start.

And when you always expect to lose, it's hard not to quit before you start.

The flip side of perfectionism, albeit springing from the exact same source, is quitterism, aka low expectations, aka resignation, aka *I give up.* Perfectionists drive themselves be-yond reason to compensate for their "inadequacy." Quitters are paralyzed beyond reason by their "inadequacy." The myth of inadequacy drives both extremes, both of which have upsides: Perfectionists gain success when they win. Quitters never lose, technically speaking, because they never compete. But when it comes to getting stuff done, perfectionists have the edge over quitters. Asked to cross the booby-trapped landscape leading to self-acceptance, quitters quit.

Some of us aim low, lower, lowest, then stop aiming alto-gether. Some of us haven't taken aim in a very long time.

On the day of the annual Hacienda Club swimming races, six small girls stood side by side at the edge of the pool, waiting to dive. The summer sky burned blue behind their heads. Their parents, friends, and fellow club members watched from lounge chairs, sipping drinks.

Next up, shouted the emcee. *One lap. Six- and seven-year-old girls.*

I was one of those girls, but I was eight. I knew this. Mom knew. She had signed me up for this race instead of the one I should have swum: one lap, eight- and nine-year-old girls.

That race, she reasoned, I might lose.

Thus I swam against smaller, younger, weaker girls.

Thus I learned to aim low.

And even then I did not win.

And thus I learned to quit.

Mom knew I was a good swimmer. But fearing failure—mine, which would reflect on her—she hedged our bets.

Having enrolled ten-year-old me in a baking class that ended with a contest among cakes we girls had ostensibly baked at home, she baked my cake.

Cheating? What? Morality never even entered into the equation. To her, it wasn't about cheating. It was simply a desperate attempt to avoid public humiliation.

I was not born for contests. Solitary, passive, lazy, I dislike teamwork and waiting. Worst of all, I disappear when judged.

I learned from her: never compete with anyone unless you know for sure that you will win. Which is to say: never compete, because you can never be sure of anything.

The world eagerly welcomes quitters. The fewer of us in the race, the better *their* chances to win.

A letter that the French novelist Gustave Flaubert sent to a friend while traveling in Egypt elucidates the hopelessness that drives even the best and the brightest to quitterism:

"I go dreaming into the future, where I see nothing, nothing. I have no plans, no idea, no project, and, what is worse, no ambition. Something—the eternal 'what's the use?'—sets its bronze barrier across every avenue that I open up in the realm of hypothesis. . . . I should like to know the source of the profound disgust that fills me these days."

Low self-esteem and aiming low—they go together. Like the chicken and the egg. But in this crowded world, everything is a kind of contest: Jobs. Relationships. Appearance. Health. Status. Success. Quitting shields us from sharp edges. Quitters settle for whatever.

What made us quit? Some were berated for their failures. Some saw that their wins and losses mattered too much to their spellcasters. Some froze in fear. Some say: *Why bother? I was born to lose.*

HOW TO DISMANTLE THIS BOOBY TRAP

We have nothing to prove. Like everyone, sometimes we win, sometimes we lose. Once we can grasp these basic facts, striving for a goal need not become a life-or-death crisis. Confucius said, "It does not matter how slowly you go as long as you do not stop." That's a variation on "It's not about whether you win or lose; it's how you play the game." But quitterism is the opposite of understanding that we sometimes win and sometimes lose and should just play games. It's the opposite of perseverance. Quitterism is another name for not even trying. It could be easily mistaken for sloth. It's also the only way to ensure that you will not win.

Self-loathing makes us dread being seen as losers. By quitting, we imagine that there's no way to lose, because when we quit we aren't in life's game at all. But the truth is devastating: By quitting, we also guarantee that we will never be winners either. And someone who never wins is, by definition, a loser. End of story. End of many, many stories.

Quitterism is just another coping mechanism to deflect the pain of hating oneself and having that hatred validated, *mandated*, by calculable loss.

But quitterism is also the opposite of curiosity. In Sophie Kinsella's novel *Remember Me?*, a young woman wakes up in a hospital bed after a car accident only to realize that she has lost all memory of the previous three years. Returning to her former workplace, exhausted and confused, "I staggered into the kitchen, made a cup of tea with three spoonfuls of sugar, then sat down and wrote out on a sheet of paper, wincing at every movement:

OPTIONS

1. *Give up.*

2. *Don't give up.*

"I stared at it for ages. Then at last I put a line through *Give up.*

"The thing with giving up is you never know. You never know whether you could have done the job. And I'm sick of not knowing about my life."

Don't *you* want to know? Cross out *Give up.*

Booby Trap #8: Loyalty

Emily is careful to never badmouth her big sister Pat. While recounting some horrifying quote or anecdote—*Pat threw away the birthday gift I made her, Pat says normal guys will never like me, Pat booed during my cello reutal, Pat says my lips are my only decent feature*—Emily keeps her large brown eyes resolutely blank. Then she shudders. You can literally see guilt racing down her spine, guilt at badmouthing her sister. Emily looks away, as if she doesn't know where those words came from, or who said them, as if she would give anything to take them back.

And if you say: *That's horrible,* Emily stiffens.

Pat didn't mean it THAT way, Emily demurs. *Pat gets terrible migraines. And guess what? She pays my rent.*

Her eyes beg you to fight for her, to say what she cannot. But at the same time, her eyes warn in no uncertain terms: *Shut up.*

Emily knows her sister is outrageous. She knows her sister is mean. She knows, oh yes she knows. Why else would she invoke those quotes and anecdotes? She is too smart to let them spill by accident. She wants a witness. She wants *you* to rage while she sits mildly by, feigning surprise.

We pledged allegiance. Signed our vows in blood. How can we break that bond?

In 1978, crazed cult leader Jim Jones persuaded nearly a thousand of his followers to drink deadly cyanide-spiked punch in a South American jungle. Spouses fed each other the punch. Parents fed it to their children. *That* was loyalty.

Few of us were ever asked to display our fealty with such finality. But we who hate ourselves can be lethally loyal nonetheless. Even if we never convulse in a jungle with 912 moribund pals as Jones and his cultists did, we *could* ruin our lives hewing to the dictates of those who crushed our self-esteem.

Yet even as we obey our spellcasters, we deny that this is even happening.

We deny this because the contracts by which our souls were sundered said: *Thou shalt forget.*

"The initial symbiotic relationship between mother and child" is a wellspring of loyalty, wrote abuse expert and psychoanalyst Alice Miller. "This early conditioning makes it virtually impossible for the child to discover what is actually happening to him. The child's dependence on his or her parents' love also makes it impossible in later years to recognize these traumatizations, which often remain hidden behind the early idealization of the parents for the rest of the child's life."

Thus the children of a cruel father *"must not* hate their father—this [is] the message of the Fourth Commandment," Miller added. "They *cannot* hate him either, if they must fear losing his love as a result; finally, they do not even *want* to hate him, because they love him. Thus, children, unlike concentration-camp inmates, are confronted by a tormentor they love, not one they hate."

We are born begging to be loyal.

"Every child has an urgent need for good parenting," writes *Soul Murder* author Leonard Shengold, "and this makes him or her cling desperately to whatever fragments of realistic benevolent parental functioning exist and to what is frequently the *delusion* of having had a concerned, loving parent."

Thus like cultists defending their supreme leaders, we often defend our spellcasters—whether they are our parents or other people who had power over us—against dissent from everyone, even ourselves. We shield them by blaming *ourselves* for their misdeeds. We do this by obeying their implicit and explicit orders: starving, slashing, drugging, and denying ourselves because they said we were ugly, unworthy, and must prove our love. Or because we think this somehow comforts them.

Mom hated herself and was terrified of everything. To be loyal, I had to hate myself and be terrified too. To be brave and not hate myself was treason. I saw her pain and there, with the grace of God, went I.

One night I, as a tiny child in frilly skirt and orthopedic shoes, was given in a seafood restaurant a promotional toy clown. Later I cuddled it in bed, addressing it aloud. Mom pounded down the hall into my room, asking to whom I was talking. I said no one, which, the toy clown not being human, was partially true. Flinging away my blanket, she saw the clown in my arms.

Liars are worse than thieves, she said in her steel-wheels-on-gravel voice. *You might as well have stabbed me with a knife.*

I wept. I was a criminal. To disobey is to betray.

But love sweet love and loyalty is this:

Year upon year I shared her fears. I shared her tears, adding oceansful of my own to seal the deal. Just as, in Greek mythology, Herakles aided Atlas by bearing the burden of the heavens on his shoulders, I took it as my task to lessen her bone-shattering load of fear and pain and vigilance and dread. As if to say: *See? Here we are, together, facing off the murderers and accidents and jerks!*

As she sometimes said: *You and me against the world.*

Fast-forward many years that, no, I will never get back.

Freedom and laughter feel to me subversive. Shafts of optimism look like theft. Standing here now, wanting—for me, for her—to sap the spells and snap the chains feels like abandonment, like burning down her house and squirting acid in her eyes. This is my loyalty. *I might as well have stabbed her with a knife.*

She did not ask for this. Not *this.* As she grew more and more depressed, she *did* ask me to murder her, to end her sorrows in this world. She asked me this as you might ask someone to have a picnic, with a luster in her eyes that might, in a book, illustrate the word *eureka*. I refused. I told her life was sacred and I did not want to go to jail. I told her (true) I have recurring nightmares about being on trial. *Oh great,* she snorted as you might at someone who refused to wash a dish. Then she went back to gazing over my shoulder as usual.

She did not ask me to become a hypochondriac, although I did. She asked me only to believe her when she said the world was absolutely, truly terrifying and I did. I do. I am loyal. *No one gets out of here alive.*

HOW TO DISMANTLE THIS BOOBY TRAP

When Steven Hassan joined Reverend Sun Myung Moon's Unification Church, he and his fellow Moonies were indoctrinated to believe "that we would be betraying God, the Messiah, ten generations of our ancestors—the whole world, in fact—if we ever left. We were told that all of our relatives now in the spirit world would accuse us throughout eternity for betraying God. It was quite a heavy trip."

Leaving the cult two years later felt at first like a terrible act of disloyalty against not just Reverend Moon—whom Hassan had addressed as "True Father"—but also God, the Messiah, and his own ancestors. Hassan began to recover only after realizing that he had been a victim of mind control.

Once he accepted this fact, Hassan resolved to learn as much as possible about mind control—the process, its effects, its perpetrators, and its victims throughout history: The more he read, the stronger and less alone he felt. Disarm this booby trap by doing as the bumper stickers say: question authority.

Mom would be shocked today to know the whole of it, to read the roster of my lamentations. Wouldn't she?

But does it matter? What purpose do our loyalties serve anymore? What does it matter what our spellcasters would think if they could see us now, if they could read our minds as they assured us that they could? What does it matter now, especially if those to whom we pledged our loyalty are lost in time and space, thousands of miles away or dead?

It matters not. The Kool-Aid contains cyanide. No one is forcing you to drink. This much you know.

Booby Trap #9: Doubt

Also known as having no confidence.

Also known as belief in our unworthiness. Incompetence. Inferiority.

Also known as *I can't*.

How can we stop hating ourselves if we think hatred toward us—ours and everyone's—is justified?

How can we free ourselves if we think we deserve captivity?

How can we help ourselves if we think we deserve no help?

How can we hope for better days when we are without hope? We can't.

The trouble with self-loathing is that it feels real. It makes us *believe* we *are* stupid, worthless, ugly, evil, and otherwise bad, thus meriting all punishment. Victory? Freedom? What? For *us?!* Be brave? Grow up? Release regret? Be independent? Never quit? We can't.

We can't, can't, can't, can't, can't. Whatever our perceived faults, we are brilliant at one thing at least: making up reasons why we *can't*. I can't look good when I go out because I can't stop eating doughnuts and I can't stop not wanting to exercise and I can't choose flattering outfits because I can't elevate my taste and I can't choose anything anyway and even if I could, I can't afford better clothes because I can't get a better job because I can't look good when I go out. I can't turn over a new post–self-loathing leaf and smile today because people will say: *That's fake, you never smiled before.* I can't say unflattering things about my parents because who does that? Only the very, very, very bad. Plus I could have done more for Mom in her last years. I could have—should have?—moved back in with her. I said: *I can't,* and having said *I can't,* can I now say her last years were okay? I can't. Thus I can't saunter blithely into my tomorrows, I can't keep pretending to be human, I can't write this book.

This booby trap afflicts us with what I—not lightly, as a hypochondriac—call *can'tser.*

Can't proceed because I lack the knowledge, beauty, skills, will, courage, character. Can't change because I never have. Can't win because I always lose.

It hurts, cripples, and kills.

Although we have by now unpacked the baseless origins of our self-loathing, we were spellbound for so long that we doubt our ability, our rights, our permission to travel on. We doubt that we can or should escape booby traps. We doubt that we will reach the Land Beyond, much less succeed in it. We doubt our very presence in the first place. *Am I real?*

The trouble with self-loathing is—self-loathing. We resign ourselves to resignation. In a series of studies, researchers played mournful music to induce a "sad mood" in people with high self-esteem and people with low self-esteem. Both groups were then offered a selection of videos to watch afterward. Some of these videos were depressing and some were cheery. Nearly twice as many high-self-esteem people as low-self-esteem people made a cheery choice.

"People with low self-esteem feel resignation because they question whether anything will help. [They] say, 'I'm not good at breaking or changing a mood.' They also believe sadness is not something you get rid of and that you learn and grow from sadness," said the lead researcher. "They feel it is not appropriate to try to change a mood." They think they *can't*.

A lifetime of self-loathing has so etched my brain that I *still* believe I can't—literally, as in lacking ability, and figuratively, as in being legally prohibited—move on. Was I granted a glint of self-acceptance by mistake, because some sentinel mistook me for someone else, someone good whose gait resembles mine or who has identical ears? Did I get this far by the grace of a double-crossing deity who will have the last laugh by showing me how lovely life can be before hurling me back into the abyss?

We shrug in resignation, thinking not only *I can't,* but also *You can't*:

You can't understand. You can't forgive me. You can't love me. You can't want to be with me. You can't encourage me. So stop.

My blood runs cold. Really it does. Right now. It runs cold

at the prospect of un-punishment. Of simply striding free. My blood runs cold at the idea of escape. Forgiveness. Grace.

HOW TO DISMANTLE THIS BOOBY TRAP

At first glance, doubt appears to be the direct opposite of hope and faith and love. Doubt—and *can'tser*—seem to devour all positive emotions in their deadly path.

But doubt, hope, love, and faith are "only" feelings, all equally mutable and flexible. Imagine the phrase *I can't* as a leaf that has flown into your hair on a windy day. Imagine plucking that leaf from your hair, holding it in your palm, and letting the wind take it back, blow it away. Look, other feelings are swirling past you now, some lighting on your shoulders. Petals. Hope, faith, love.

Like so much else about self-loathing, *can'tser* takes what could be helpful to toxic extremes. It's good to know our limitations. Good to know our strengths and weaknesses, our deficits and skills. How laughable are tone-deaf howlers who fly into rages when rejected during TV talent shows. Doubt can be a strategic tool, applied clear-eyedly and honestly. This is the difference between standing at the edge of the Grand Canyon, behind a guardrail, and jumping in.

"Your doubt can become a good quality if you *train* it," Rainer Maria Rilke wrote in a letter to a young fan who sought his advice. "It must become *knowing*, it must become criticism. Ask it, whenever it wants to spoil something for you, *why* something is ugly, demand proofs from it, test it, and you will find it perhaps bewildered and embarrassed, perhaps also protesting. But don't give in, insist on arguments, and act in this way, attentive and persistent, every single time, and the day will come when, instead of being a destroyer, it will become one of your best workers—perhaps the most intelligent of all the ones that are building your life."

We must not mistake our doubts for certainty. We must not read our doubts as permission slips to quit. Rather, we must accept that doubts are intrinsically human. The very existence of *I can't* mandates the presence of its opposite, the magnetic pole of *I can.* Faith and doubt face each other, reflect on each other, dare each other. Intrinsic in the depths of doubt is the pull of the other "pole." Let yourself feel that pull.

Booby Trap #10: Self-Criticism

Sticks and stones can break our bones. But words—said to ourselves from the depths of hatred—hurt us too.

Scripts our spellcasters made us memorize we now recite as if they were our own, spontaneous, and true.

Mom signed her letters to me "Fatmom," scribbling next to this word a "self-portrait": a circle with arms and legs. She was not fat, not that it mattered to me. But it mattered to her.

We tell ourselves terrible things.

"O, what a rogue and peasant slave am I! . . . / A dull and muddy-mettled rascal," fumes Prince Hamlet:

John-a-dreams, unpregnant of my cause,
And can say nothing; no. . . .
Am I a coward? . . .
I am pigeon-liver'd and lack gall. . . .
Why, what an ass am I!

You might be guilty of equally outrageous self-criticism. Which words, what grammar do you use when speaking to and of yourself? What if your every word and thought was secretly recorded every day by some miraculous device, which nightly forced you to review its gleanings?

How shocked would you be to see and hear such contempt? How astounded would you be at your own self-absorption, the negative narcissism of the ruthless inner critic? How stunned would you be to hear yourself sound like a sadist, rapist, bully, psychopath, or prison guard?

Negative self-talk is addictive. Like other addictions, it starts small and soothes, at least at first. Cruel words were the words some of us always knew best. Repeating and reciting them was hypnotically comforting, because like lullabies they were familiar and, perversely, felt like home.

We *mean* these nasty words. They are reflexive, inadvertent, nonchalant, perfunctory—but to us they are true. Thus saying them feels no more harrowing or dire than tying shoes and signing checks. But what if every time you signed a check or tied a shoe it left a scar?

Negative self-talk is like puncturing oneself with pins, or tripping oneself—again and again. *Ouch. Ha! Oof. Ha! Ouch.* We are puncturer and punctured, tripped and tripper, unable to outsmart or escape ourselves. We are determined to attack the easiest of targets: us.

Kind words said to ourselves would sound foreign and feel like mutiny. Disloyalty.

What was your first hating word? When did you say it, where, and why?

One of my first memories is Mom gazing into the bedroom mirror, poking herself in the face, and whispering:

Fat pig.

Fat ugly pig.

Having just learned to speak, I thought: *This is what ladies say.* I knew no other ladies. Looking into mirrors, I copied her words just as, playing tea party with my toys, I copied her gestures and wore her hats.

Children learn languages that way. Self-loathing has a lexicon. Every time we ponder taking a step toward self-acceptance, our inner critic stands in our way, arms crossed, sneering: *Where do you think you're going, fool?*

HOW TO DISMANTLE THIS BOOBY TRAP

We've heard this cliché countless times: *Stop putting yourself down!* But how? Changing the way we talk to ourselves means changing the way we think about ourselves. A good goal, but it cannot happen overnight.

Positive affirmations work for some. For others, not so much.

In one study, a group of people with low self-esteem and a group of people with high self-esteem were instructed to repeat the affirmation *I am a lovable person.* Both groups were asked to describe their feelings about themselves both before and after repeating the affirmation. The people with high self-esteem felt better about themselves after repeating the affirmation. The people with low self-esteem *felt significantly worse about themselves after repeating the affirmation*. Another group of people with low self-esteem was not instructed to repeat the affirmation. This last group remained emotionally unchanged—feeling no worse about themselves at the end of the experiment than they had felt when it began. Only those people with low self-esteem who had said "I am a lovable person" felt worse at the end of the experiment.

"Repeating positive self-statements may benefit certain people," the researchers concluded, but can "backfire for the very people who need them the most."

Dishonestly repeating an untrue "affirmation" feels to us who hate ourselves like simply one more form of faking it: Before this experiment, we were just ugly losers. After the experiment, we're ugly losers who also lie.

To some of us, affirmations sound too silly and grandiose to believe or say, much less internalize.

Kristin Neff, an associate professor of human development and culture at the University of Texas and the author of *Self-Compassion: Stop Beating Yourself Up and Leave Insecurity Behind*, suggests that instead of trying to debate or denounce our inner critics, we should accept and respect them:

However hurtful its words, "our self-critic is trying to keep us safe. It's trying to give us a protective message—'Watch out! You might be rejected! You might be left alone! You might mess up!' No matter what the self-critic says and no matter where in our childhood it learned to say these things, its driving desire is to keep us safe"—as is that of the false self proposed by D. W. Winnicott.

Neff advises talking compassionately to your inner critic. "Try telling it: 'Thank you! I see how hard you're trying to help me. But is there another way I can feel safe besides hearing your messages?'

"Until you accept it and understand it, the self-critic will feel angry and ignored, like its message isn't being heard, like it has something to say and you won't listen. Once it knows that you know it means well, it starts to loosen its grip."

CHAPTER 4

The Upside of Low Self-Esteem

The whole problem with the world is that fools and
fanatics are always so certain of themselves, and
wiser people so full of doubts.

—BERTRAND RUSSELL

The young woman sitting across from me on the train is talking on the phone. *Fucking professor gave me a fucking B-plus,* she snarls, crossing her legs. *I marched into his fucking office after class and said, Give me an A. I mean, who does he think he fucking IS?*

The strappy skintight top and short shorts she is wearing do not flatter her. I think she does not realize this. It's not like some people who know that certain outfits do not flatter them but wear those outfits anyway, rebelliously. I think she *really does not know.*

My mom wants me to get a summer job, she says into the phone. *I know! Fuck that! Like I would stand there frying fries. As IF.*

She hangs up, applies lipstick, makes kissy faces while taking pictures of herself. The train pulls to a stop, causing a man to brush against her knees as he limps past on crutches. *Watch it!* she yells, rubbing her knees as if they have been slimed.

If that's high self-esteem, then maybe I would rather keep mine low.

Is low self-esteem all that bad? Self-loathing is. But between self-loathing and narcissism is a vast spectrum comprising infinitely various degrees of self-regard. Neither extreme is good. If only we could just reach medium.

We know we don't want to end up like that young woman on the train—insulting, condescending, deluded, entitled. We don't want to become egomaniacs like Jean-Baptiste Clamence, the narrator of Albert Camus' novel *The Fall*, who declares:

"I have to admit it. . . . I, I, I is the refrain of my whole life, which could be heard in everything I said. I could never talk without boasting, especially if I did so with that shattering discretion that was my specialty . . . for the excellent reason that I recognized no equals. I always considered myself more intelligent than everyone else . . . but also more sensitive and more skillful, a crack shot, an incomparable driver, a better lover. Even in the fields in which it was easy for me to verify my inferiority—like tennis, for instance, in which I was but a passable partner—it was hard for me not to think that, with a little time and practice, I would surpass the best players. I admitted only superiorities in me. . . . When I was concerned with others, I was so out of pure condescension . . . and all the credit went to me: my self-esteem would go up a degree."

In 1986, California State Assemblymember John Vasconcellos proposed the State Task Force to Promote Self-Esteem. This ignited a new movement: Based on the notion that low self-esteem caused every kind of social woe from teenage pregnancy to low test scores and high dropout rates, school curricula and parenting techniques were radically transformed, their main objective now being to cultivate high self-esteem among the young, which activists proclaimed would cure those social woes and make America a safer, happier, and better place. A multibillion-dollar industry surged around self-esteem. Kids were taught to make "me" flags of their putative "me" nations, to view history and fiction through the filter of their *feelings*, and to start schooldays with affirmations such as *I always make good choices* and *Everyone is happy to see me*.

The aftermath has not worked out as planned. Since 1986, self-esteem among young people *has* increased. Studies show that students hold themselves in higher regard than students in decades past. But to the shock and horror of the self-esteem movement's boosters, soaring self-esteem has done nothing to stem crime, addiction, and those other ills the boosters claimed high self-esteem would stem. In fact, ambient sky-high self-esteem might present new problems of its own: one long-term study found that college students are now twice as narcissistic as college students were in 1982; other studies link high self-esteem with high rates of aggression, territorialism, elitism, racism, and other negative qualities.

And other studies show that the so-called Millennial Generation—young adults born after the self-esteem movement began—are demonstrably less likely than baby boomers and Generation Xers to care about social problems, current events, or energy conservation. Millennials are also less likely to have jobs whose main purpose is to help other people. In one study, three times as many Millennials as baby boomers said they made no personal effort to help the environment.

"Certain forms of high self-esteem seem to increase one's proneness to violence," reads one report published in the journal of the American Psychological Association. "An uncritical endorsement of the cultural value of high self-esteem may therefore be counterproductive and even dangerous. The societal pursuit of high self-esteem for everyone may literally end up doing considerable harm."

Noting that there are "almost no findings showing that [high] self-esteem causes anything [beneficial] at all," University of Pennsylvania psychology professor Martin Seligman laments:

"Something striking has happened to the self-esteem of American children during the era of raising our children to feel good. They have never been more depressed."

This is no doubt partly because, raised to believe that they are special and perfect and entitled to all good things, they face terrible comedowns in the real world.

If (as often happens nowadays) every student in a class gets an A grade or every player in a tournament gets a trophy not because they all deserved these things, but rather in order to boost their self-esteem, then A becomes commonplace and meaningless, an average grade of no particular pride-inducing significance, just as C was a few decades ago. And the notion of "victory" is blurred. If *everyone* is special, then *no one* is special. QED.

Such revelations might shock the self-esteem boosters, who envisioned high self-esteem as an all-powerful magic potion, but will probably not shock *us*. Researchers have found that high self-esteem does not guarantee happiness and is often linked with depression because those whose self-esteem is elevated on false or flimsy pretexts—e.g., being told that everyone adores you or being told you're perfect just for *existing*—are highly susceptible to all perceived slights. So-called beneficiaries of the self-esteem boom have been brainwashed to believe they deserve the best grades, the best treatment, the best of everything. Thus they are very easily offended, angered, disappointed, and crushed by even the faintest criticism. Psychologists call *that* kind of sky-high but baseless self-esteem "fragile self-esteem." Its healthy opposite is achievement-based "secure self-esteem"—otherwise known as *earned* self-*respect*—which is not necessarily sky-high, but closer to medium, and less likely to leave its possessors sulking and raging when the real world delivers its usual harsh doses of reality.

People with high self-esteem often seem like aliens to us, and icky aliens at that. We blame ourselves for everything. They take no blame. We're always sorry. They never are. We fear punishment. They don't. Often, they do the punishing. Our flaws obsess us. They think they have none.

"One has only to go into a prison," writes former jail doctor Theodore Dalrymple, "to see the most revoltingly high self-esteem among a group of people (the young thugs) who had brought nothing but misery to those around them, largely because they conceived of themselves as so important that they could do no wrong. For them, their whim was law, which was precisely as it should be considering who they were in their own estimate."

But see, *we could have told you that.*

A comprehensive review of self-esteem research published in the journal of the Association for Psychological Science in 2003 is titled "Does High Self-Esteem Cause Better Performance, Interpersonal Success, Happiness, or Healthier Lifestyles?"

According to its authors, a team of professors from major universities, the answer is no, no, no, and no.

"Our findings do not support continued widespread efforts to boost self-esteem in the hope that it will by itself foster improved outcomes," the authors warn. In fact, "indiscriminate praise might just as easily promote narcissism, with its less desirable consequences."

They recommend instead that high self-esteem be promoted not as a basic birthright but rather as a goal attained through achievements and ethical behavior. (*Hey, why did no one ever think of this before? Oh wait, they did. It was how every culture on Earth functioned until a few years ago.*) In other words, *feeling* good should stem from *doing* good.

"After all, Hitler had very high self-esteem," the authors note. "He attracted followers by offering them self-esteem that was not tied to achievement or ethical behavior—rather, he told them that they were superior beings simply by virtue of being themselves, members of the so-called Master Race, an idea that undoubtedly had a broad, seductive appeal."

Self-loathing and narcissism are both unhealthy because both are forms of self-absorption, albeit at opposite extremes. Whether we are always sorry or never sorry, *it is all about us.*

Most spiritual paths advocate a conscientious middle ground. According to these doctrines, good people just do good, which generally entails neither playing God nor playing dead.

According to the *Tao Te Ching*, a sage "does not consider himself right, and thus is illustrious. He does not brag, and thus has merit. . . . The sage knows himself but does not display himself."

A sage, the *Tao Te Ching* asserts, emulates water:

"Nothing in the world is as soft and gentle as water. Yet it has great strength. It flows downhill and can easily wear away the hardest stone. The soft and gentle can conquer the hard and firm."

In Christian tradition, pride is not just one of the Seven Deadly Sins, but is considered the worst sin of all, a mortal sin, and the cause of all others. The original term for this sin was not "pride" but the Greek word *hubris*, which some scholars say should be more accurately translated as "unmerited high self-esteem." For two thousand years in the Western world, high self-esteem or pride was considered a moral failing yet now children are brought up believing that it's the highest virtue.

Spiritual texts laud the modest and the humble. "The palace pillar is wide, but the human heart should be modest," reads a Shinto poem. "The inhabitants of Paradise will be all the humble and the weak," reads Islam's Hadith of Bukhari. "Be humble; be harmless; have no pretension," urges the Hindu Bhagavad Gita.

Modesty is not shame but decorum. Humility is not self-abasement but respect.

"Beware of practicing your righteousness before other people in order to be seen by them, for then you will have no reward from your Father," warns the New Testament's Book of Matthew. "When pride comes, then comes disgrace, but with humility is wisdom," notes the Book of Proverbs. Saint Augustine observed: "There can only be two basic loves: The love of God unto the forgetfulness of self, or the love of self unto the forgetfulness and denial of God."

Through a practice known as *bodhicitta*, devout Buddhists pledge to spread compassion through the world, aiming to end the suffering of "all sentient beings." The funny thing that happens in the midst of all this liberating, shimmering compassion is that somewhere down the road, you realize that all sentient beings include you.

Low self-esteem does not enlighten us. Self-loathing is not holy. But, all else aside, low self-esteem makes us contemplative and introspective. Our perfectionism makes us diligent. We celebrate small pleasures—albeit because we believe ourselves unworthy of big ones. We try hard. We aim to please. Low self-esteem makes some of us creative—as we seek meaning in pain. Low self-esteem makes some of us respectful—because we assume everyone is better than us. Low self-esteem makes some of us gentle—because we are not strong. Low self-esteem makes some of us hilarious—because self-deprecating humor is humor indeed. Low self-esteem makes some of us good listeners—because we do not want to listen to ourselves. Low self-esteem makes some of us empathic—because we have suffered, so we know.

. . .

We who hate ourselves are not saints. And yet self-loathing—in spite of itself—has given us gifts that we get to keep.

CHAPTER 5

What Works for You: Seven Healing Strategies

The eyes of others our prisons; their thoughts our cages.

—VIRGINIA WOOLF

Certain schools of therapy hold that universal archetypes apply to everyone, but not all of us with low self-esteem conceptualize our struggles in exactly the same way. Depending on our histories and personalities, self-loathing makes some of us feel like prisoners. Others see self-loathing as a sickness or a disability or a disorder. Self-loathing makes some of us feel as if we have been brainwashed, recruited into an evil cult. Some of us feel like puppets. Paper dolls. Trained seals. Some of us feel spellbound, pricked with poisoned barbs. Mesmerized. Cursed.

This chapter presents seven healing strategies based on seven different powerful metaphors. Which ones are the most powerful for you? Which might provide the emotional tools you need to pull you through?

Find Your Place

There is a place where you'd hate yourself less.

Somewhere out there, it waits. Each of us has one, whether we know it or not, whether we have found it or not, whether we have seen it with our own eyes or not. It is a nation or a city block, a mountain or a room. It is the Mekong Delta or the Prado, shopping malls or Prague. It is highly specific and one-of-a-kind—a certain park, say, or a certain cinema—or else it is not a place but a type of place: caves, say, or hole-in-the-wall Chinese restaurants. In the latter case, two caves, one in Laos and one in Canada, or two hole-in-the-wall Chinese restaurants, one in Rome and one in Shanghai, are equally your place.

Maybe you already know where it is, the place where you hate yourself less. Maybe you go there every March. Or maybe you know where it is and yet have never been there in the flesh.

Or maybe you have no idea that such a place exists. It does. The formula for finding it is simple:

1. *What makes you hate yourself?*

2. *Where do those things occur least?*

3. *What makes you feel inspired, serene, amused, excited (in a good way), unself-conscious, passionate, compassionate, and more or less at home?*

4. *Where are those things?*

For me, it is the seashore.

I know: the sea kills. But I hate myself less beside the sea—oh any sea, not bay or harbor but actual rolling, splashing sea: not in or on the sea but near enough on solid ground to see, hear, smell, and feel it, the wilder the better, preferably in sight of boats. Thinking of seashores fevers me with yearning, tinged with shame because yearning is one more thing that makes me hate myself. I do not want to say how much I miss the shore, because if someone finds out, they might take my place away.

I know: some people hate the sea. I knew someone who was so traumatized by childhood seaside trips as to despise the sight and sound of surf forevermore. She shuddered at the shriek of gulls. But, as do all of us, she had a place where she loathed herself less. It was the gift shop where she worked for forty years amid beautiful merchandise, coworkers who respected her, and customers who thanked her. I know someone else who hates himself least at ice-skating rinks. He likes the gentle rinkside etiquette. He likes belonging to a crowd of happy strangers, meeting their eyes as they pass. He likes, as all the world outside the rink stands still, to glide. He likes his thighs.

And granted: Some of us who hate ourselves believe that they would hate themselves anywhere, everywhere. And some of us who hate ourselves believe that they hate themselves least in places where they barely feel at all. Some believe that they hate themselves least in dangerous places where they dare themselves moment by moment not to die.

I prefer wild, deserted coasts. For me, the shore is not a people place. It does not ask our names. It tolerates our presence restively. It would not mind, it would not notice, if we disappeared.

The sea expects nothing from me. I cannot disappoint the sea. It does not care. It does not hate me, does not love me, does not wonder who I am or what I wear, because it does not care whether I am or am not there. The sea roars, either way. This not-caring, this panoramic cannot-care amidst the lambent sheen of sand and spray is glorious because people who claimed to care about me made me (in the name of caring) hate myself. It was people who, while I cuddled plastic-headed toys, told me that I must never lie. Then, folding their arms and crossing their legs, they lied.

The sea does none of this, because it is the sea. Its inhumanity is an unwitting generosity. We cannot be made to hate ourselves by what cannot care.

I lived beside the sea for two years, long ago. I saw it through the window of my sixth-floor room and walked its warm sand every day. Then with the easy-come-easy-go gluttony of college girls, I left that paradise as if I might someday be back. But no, never: not to that exact patch of sacred sand.

I also like the desert. Forest. Field. I prefer seashores because they are wet, because like perpetual treasure hunts they are strewn with jewels to find, because their creatures like to dive, because their crashing makes me think in rhyme.

But that's just me. And here is where the last half of our formula comes into play. The place where you hate yourself less is not merely a concordance of negatives, holy only for what it lacks, is not, and cannot do. The place where you hate yourself less inspires and cheers you for what it has, is, and does.

Find your place. Optimally, go there. If you cannot—yet—then look at pictures of it. Listen to recordings of its noises. Think of it. What is it about this place that makes you hate yourself less?

I ask because your answers are about more than a place. These places exist. They are real. Inhabiting them in the flesh, breathing their air, can heal. But even just one weekend there, or even just a fantasy, vouchsafes a vital taste of how hating ourselves less feels. That strange, sudden serenity. That mandibular ease. That lightness in hands, feet, and eyes is possible, and once we taste it, by the sea or in the bowling alley, we will know. And we can fight—against whatever made us hate ourselves, against those relics of our histories, against those voices in our heads that sound like us warning *No no no no*—never to let it go.

Break Out of Your Inner Prison: The Jailer Has Departed

This is how our mornings sounded:

Don't close the bathroom door when I'm talking to you. What do you mean, this is embarrassing? I changed your diapers once upon a time. How are your bowels? Are you slouching strangely or is that a roll of fat?

Hurry and wipe yourself or we'll be late. What if Miss Rose gives a pop quiz today? Focus. Don't sit there like a dummy thinking about pissy little boys.

Oh hell, it looks like rain. Oh hell hell hell. You'll catch pneumonia. Seat belt! Want to fly straight through the windshield if some bastard smacks us? Want to die right here on Western Avenue?

Here we are at school. Look—your friends are laughing at you. Why? Is it your clothes or—? Probably. Bitches! Bye-bye. I love you. Love me? Say so. Smile. I said smile. God, your teeth. They just get browner every day.

It was not horrible. It was not child abuse. It was no worse—far nicer, really—than the things Mom told herself. Well-meaning monologues, spontaneously scathing. This was simply how she thought. She never guessed that, decades hence, I would be terrified of accidents, illness, and nearly everything my body did. She never guessed that her words would stick in my mind just as the schoolboys' barks stuck in my friend Bettina's mind and Emily could not forget the booing of her sister Pat. Hearing such commentary so continuously made it sound like birdsong: unintrusive, ambient, appropriate, correct, its content no more to be questioned or protested than you would question or protest cooing doves. Its absence would have felt sudden, surreal, a dull silence like sickness. But that silence never came, because it never stopped.

But then it did, because I left home. *But I called Mom from college three times a day, as if I had to hear it, had to had to had to.* It was reassurance. It was guidance. It was love. Then, much later, it stopped for sure, because she died.

I have not heard it, really *heard* it with my outside-ears, for years. And yet I hear it with my inside-ears: Mom's monologue, which all my life I have mistaken for my thoughts.

I was a prisoner in someone else's world. In someone else's

fear. In someone else's madness. In someone else's self-loathing. *My self-loathing isn't even mine.*

I was condemned. I was confined. I was incarcerated in her misery and thus I am incarcerated in this story. Do you think I want to tell this story, tell it yet again, the Ancient Mariner in sneakers and a sweatshirt, ranting: *Mom did this* and *Dad did that?* I don't. I want not to be telling it, I want never to have told it, I want never to have needed to tell it. I wish I was writing a grown-up book as grown-up writers do, not *whine whine whine* about Mommy and Daddy *still*, not telling this story but other stories not involving them, stories in which their faces do not loom like big frowning balloons above my head. I want to write books about normal things that people half my age write books about: chemistry, say, or spies or—I don't know, Tasmania. I want to stop telling this story, shut my mouth about my parents, stop yakking about them like a stoolie, and I am so sorry, so so so sorry to still be saying this. See? I apologize to you for boring you, and I apologize to them for exposing their private lives. It never ends. But I was sentenced, and this story is my cell.

For nearly all my life, I carried my cell with me everywhere. It was invisible, even to me. At first, when I was very young, I was placed in this cell and guarded vigilantly, night and day.

But that was long ago. By now the guard has gone away.

How long have I been sitting here obediently, voluntarily, in an unguarded, unlocked cell? I cannot bear to count the decades I have spent inside this prison, which might as well have been of my own devising. And for what? The world did not become a better place thanks to my false imprisonment. My mother was not succored by my sacrifice, such as it was. To simply saunter through that open door, to "escape" now, would make my years spent behind bars seem eye-gougingly tragi-comical. Telling myself I'm still locked in makes me feel slightly less ridiculous. But then the open door swings, *creak creak creak. Regret. Fear. Can't.*

I have sawn through my chains. They lie at my feet now, rusted with age.

And yet I stay.

Prison life resembles self-loathing: Both are constant and relentless. Both condition their "inmates" to feel that they belong there.

"Years pass, and prison simply becomes the place where we live," explains Michael Powell, who served three prison terms totaling more than twenty years. "The punishment aspect fades away. We become accustomed to our environment, our world, and we even become comfortable"—so much so that the prospect of impending freedom frightens some.

"They are told to leave. They have to start all over again. Some panic. They stab another prisoner or kill one, so they will get more time. They assault guards or get caught with drugs, whatever it takes to receive a new sentence or violate their parole or lose accumulated statutory good time so they can remain in prison."

To them, "the free world is more threatening now."

Freedom can be harder than it sounds.

Mom would be horrified to hear this metaphor. She meant no harm. These things she said she thought were educational, useful, protective, like first-aid instructions or a psalm. She had a graduate degree in education from New York University. She believed she was teaching me.

Her commentary still spins in my head, albeit less than ever, now but it starts unprovoked in restaurants and clothing stores, where it always feels real at first. Then I tell it to stop. It does not always stop.

Self-loathing is my prison. Her words are its bars. All those who hate themselves know this sensation of incarceration.

Our jailers have forgotten us and left. Our cells have neither locks nor guards. But still, we need to stage a jailbreak. Here's the plan—and pass it on:

Step one: Understand that the jailers—those who locked you up—are really *gone*. Those first-grade bullies? Gone. Sadistic boyfriend? Gone. Cruel or unthinking parents? Gone. Peer pressure? Skinny models? Gone, gone, gone. They might not have been there at all after those first few terrifying moments. They hurled you into that cell, and then stationed a crude mannequin dressed as a guard next to your door and hissed, *I'll be watching you! Don't you dare move!* Then, chortling, they sauntered off to live their merry lives. They've probably forgotten you by now, just as they forgot all the other hapless souls they locked in other cells.

Step two: Test the lock, door, bars, chains. Yep. Broken. Open. Nothing is holding you back. You could walk out right now. *You could have walked out years ago.* See that sunshine out there?

Step three, the hard part: Dodge the booby traps. Don't let regret over a partly wasted life keep you imprisoned. Don't let fear of freedom make you retreat back to the illusory safety of your cell. Don't let loyalty to your long-departed jailers keep you here, in case they might return.

Ready for the jailbreak? We've done our time.

One, two, three . . .

Adopt Yourself

Looking back at my childhood self, that small figure flattening herself against walls as her inexplicably furious parents yelled at her, I want to bundle her into a blanket and whisk her away. To somewhere normal. To another life.

In other words, I want to rescue her. Free her. Re-parent her. Adopt her, if I must.

For some of us, the idea of suddenly *loving* the selves we have spent so long *hating* seems impossible. Self-love feels alien, not totally appealing, and too far a leap.

According to some compelling recent research, it's a leap in the wrong direction anyway. New studies reveal the emotional benefits not of self-love or high self-esteem but of *self-compassion*. Kindness. Comfort offered to oneself. Studies indicate that self-compassion leads to better relationships, more positive attitudes, more resilience, more optimism, higher emotional intelligence, better coping skills, stronger self-determination—and more happiness. Studies also suggest that self-compassionate people are less depressed, anxious, and narcissistic than non-self-compassionate people.

"When you feel bad, think of what you would say to a child or good friend who was suffering and say it to yourself," advises self-compassion expert Kristin Neff. "Use whatever language feels authentic—and that doesn't feel like platitudes—to tell yourself: 'I'm sorry you're going through this. My thoughts are with you.'"

We can offer compassion to our present-day selves. But our past selves need compassion too, trapped in their terrified not-knowing. If we combine self-compassion with childhood regression therapy, we get *self-adoption*. If the parenting you experienced while young damaged your self-esteem, then go back and adopt yourself and raise yourself correctly this time. Of course you can't change what really happened, but there's a secret (*shhhh*, don't tell yourself) that makes self-adoption work: while the adult you is nurturing and mentoring the metaphorical young you, it is the *adult* you who learns and grows from the experience of being a caregiver.

"We give ourselves compassion not for the sheer purpose of making ourselves feel better—not as a desperate attempt to resist, avoid, get rid of or reject some aspect of ourselves or some situation in which we find ourselves," Neff explains, "but rather to acknowledge that we're feeling bad, and to mindfully accept *what is*.

"So we offer ourselves encouragement and support."

Add a comforting squeeze or pat, just as you might give to a distressed child, "to tap into the physiology of compassion," Neff suggests. "As mammals, we calm down with warmth and a soft touch. That's universal to the mammalian system and certainly among primates. When your brain can't go straight to compassion because your brain is still full of story line and judgments, your body can lead the way into a comfort zone."

Compassion comprises three stages: First, notice that someone is suffering. Next, be verbally and physically kind and caring in response to that suffering. Third, remember that imperfection is part of the human experience.

"It's not about becoming perfect. It's about having compassion for imperfection."

Self-compassion is a great idea, but it can be devilishly hard to enact. Augmenting all those studies vaunting self-compassion are a sheaf of newer studies examining what researchers call "fear of compassion." People with low self-esteem are *afraid* to offer themselves comfort and kindness, and are even afraid of receiving compassion from others, these studies show.

Clinical psychologist Paul Gilbert, a leader in compassion-fear research, told me that this is hardly surprising:

"It's a lot easier to feel compassion toward people you like than toward people you hate."

Compassion phobia, Gilbert said, often afflicts traumatized people "for whom happiness is associated with bad things.

"They might have had unpredictable parents who might have been very punishing when their children were enjoying themselves. Or maybe someone was very happy and having a good time at the moment her husband was killed in a car crash." Traumatized as a result of their own joy, such people "feel that compassion is an indulgence they don't deserve. They believe they have to be critical, harsh and punishing toward themselves in order to ensure that they don't become lazy or arrogant."

Compassion phobia "is not an abnormal problem. It's perfectly normal. The first step is to not be critical about being critical," Gilbert advised. Recovery from compassion phobia takes time.

"If you're learning to swim, start in the shallow end. Work toward self-compassion by doing small things, nice things for yourself—I don't mean buying yourself chocolates, but going out a little farther every day into areas that formerly scared you, moving forward step by step while thinking about what you would say to a child you really loved at such times."

Compassion phobics fear that self-compassion will hurt. And they're right, Gilbert said.

"If you've felt so unworthy, so unlovable, so alone for a long time, then to realize that maybe you can feel a different way about yourself actually makes some people incredibly sad. It feels like coming home—but coming home can unleash a great deal of sorrow. It's a 'missed-you-so-much, where-have-you-been' situation."

In the park, a little girl laughs and jumps up and down as her father runs off to hide.

Where's Daddy? coos the little girl's mother, laughing too. *Where'd he go?*

Daddy! the child squeals, pigtails bouncing, knowing that she will see him, *must* see him, cannot *wait* to see him, soon soon *soon.*

The man leaps from behind a tree.

Daddy! She races to him and he picks her up. I am glad to be far away by now, because they cannot see me cry. I cry not because I never played such games with my father, but because I did.

And now I am my father and my mother, both. And I am Cara's parents, Nate's and Rachel's parents—the parents of all who hate themselves. I am the parents of the blogger whose blog is called *Gosh I Hate Myself* and who wrote, "Someone adopt me my parents are shit omfg or just help me bury their bodies cause bitches are going down if i stay with them any longer." I was not parent material when young, but at least in this fantasy I must be what my mom and dad and yours were not but could have been and almost were and either did or did not want to be.

Deprogram Yourself from the Cult of Self-Loathing

Whatever made us hate ourselves was a virtual cult.

Complete with seemingly omniscient leaders. Helpless, obedient followers. Indoctrination. Brainwashing. Trauma. Starvation. Suicide.

You and I might never have shaved our heads, chanted on street corners, or stockpiled guns in bunkers. But deprogrammers would find themselves on familiar ground if they met us.

Our spellcasters were cult leaders, using cult tactics to get cult results. Self-loathing transforms us into compliant, lying zombies: damaged half-selves who avoid eye contact and cannot say what we want.

When cult-related crimes and scandals started making headlines in the 1960s, a new industry arose around cults: researching them, rescuing and deprogramming former members, studying the psychological effects of cult membership.

Researchers determined a set of factors that define cults, regardless of type. Sexual, spiritual, survivalist, and so on, all cults share these qualities:

A cult is a group whose leader claims to be omnipotent, omniscient, supreme, and/or divine.

Cult leaders instill in cultists intense allegiance, dependence, compliance, and obedience.

In exchange for all this, cult leaders promise their followers support, security, acceptance, enlightenment, and love.

They control cultists' thoughts, emotions, and behavior.

Cult leaders divide cultists from the outside world. All people, things, and information not pertaining or belonging to the cult are denounced as inferior or evil. Contact with outsiders is controlled or banned.

Cult leaders employ what psychologists call "aversive emotional arousal techniques"—methods of mind control such as criticism, threats, blame, abuse, humiliation, and punishment.

Cultists feel incompetent, inadequate, and worthless except in their roles as devotees.

Cultists dismiss, disown, and deny their true selves.

Cultists are told that no one outside the cult loves or cares for them, or ever will.

Cultists are warned that they face capture, condemnation, and/or death if they defect.

I don't know about your childhood, but that sure as heck sounds like mine.

The people who stole our self-esteem used some of these exact same brainwashing techniques on us, with pretty much the same results. Thus we think and act in the same ways real cult members do. Don deAvila Jackson's concept of "family con-tracts" and family myths reflects this perspective. *Our* "cults" were for the most part very small: a household, a marriage, a clique—so our indoctrinations had no witnesses.

A *cult*-cult story:

Brent Jeffs was born into the Fundamentalist Church of the Latter-Day Saints, a polygamous sect disowned by the Mor-mon Church on which it modeled itself.

FLDS members were taught "perfect obedience and perfect faith. If that was not accomplished or if you did not follow ev-erything that they asked of you, then . . . you would become an apostate, which means an enemy of the church, and at the very end of it all you would be burning in hell. I mean, we were brainwashed into thinking that this was the only life to live. . . . This is black and white: You either live this life or you *have* no life. They take away everyone's choice to be who they want to be, and it's a cult because they take away free will," said Jeffs, who was raped at age five by his uncle, FLDS leader Warren Jeffs, who told the boy during the assault that it was "God's work" and "God's will."

"I thought: God hates me. God wants nothing to do with me and He's throwing me out with the trash," said Brent, who later learned that his brothers had been raped by Warren, too: one committed suicide; the other died of a drug overdose.

A self-loathing cult story:

Pat Conroy based his novel *The Great Santini* on his own life as the fearful, struggling son of a megalomaniac, a perfec-tionist fighter-pilot father who harshly punished all signs of autonomy in his wife and children:

"Ben . . . had lost count how many times he had waited beside landing strips scanning the sky for the approach of his father, his tall, jacketed father, to drop out of the sky, descending into the sight of his waiting family, a family who over the long years had developed patient eyes, sky-filled eyes, wing-blessed eyes. . . . As they ran to him, that echo from past memories rang in their brains, that password into the turbulent cellular structure of the past, the honeycomb of lost days, of laughter and fury, that told them as they ran to his outstretched arms a simple message: Lt. Col. Bull Meecham, United States Marine Corps, was back from Europe. The father had landed. The Great Santini was home."

The lucky and the brave escape. Some are rescued. Some break away—from "real" cults and from ours.

My friend Claudia, a forty-year-old rancher, had been teased relentlessly about her looks all her life when, at age nineteen, she got a marriage proposal.

"I thought: Hooray, life is good after all because this nice man loves me and thinks I'm beautiful—which proves that those bullies who teased me were wrong," Claudia remembers.

For the first two years of their marriage, "Keith totally isolated me from my family and friends, never letting me see them—or at least, never letting me see them without *him* watching over us. He had the habit of sometimes criticizing me about little things, but then he started criticizing me more and more about bigger and bigger things—like my body and major aspects of my personality.

"I didn't argue or fight with him about it. I just took it, because I was so grateful to be married and he was a fine upstanding member of the community—smart and fun and social and everyone liked him. But finally his little digs turned into unmistakable abuse. He would look me right in the eyes and call me ugly. I thought: Oh, those bullies who teased me were correct.

"I'd never had a great sense of self, but by that point it was totally *gone*. I had no idea who I was. Then one day the abuse turned physical. Keith slammed me up against a wall—and that was it. I didn't say anything, I didn't let on, but the next morning I put more stuff into my backpack than usual, hopped onto my bike, rode to work, and never went home again. I stayed with a friend and filed for divorce."

After a year mostly spent sitting at her desk and staring into space, Claudia moved to another town, had the image of a war goddess tattooed on her leg, and joined a punk rock band.

"I got into punk rock because it was angry and cathartic and that's what I needed. I changed my name because I was no longer that person who had chosen to marry Keith and who could be abused. I became a new version of myself. But it took a while to figure out who this version was."

Claudia's isolation in her abusive relationship with Keith was very similar to Brent Jeffs' isolation in FLDS: hounded, humiliated, derailed, confined, cut off from reality.

Like freed prisoners, ex-cultists find readjustment to the real world very difficult. Researchers found that ex-cultists, no matter what type of cult they have fled, tend to experience the same specific set of emotional difficulties—which can take years to resolve. In 1977, this set of symptoms was given a name: cult indoctrinee syndrome. And the symptoms are these:

CIS victims are indecisive. CIS victims are immature, childlike, or childish. CIS victims display dulled, numbed, or narrowed emotions. CIS victims find it hard to feel and express love. CIS victims find it hard to replace cultish value systems with new ones of their own. CIS victims display a lack of concern for personal hygiene and/or physical appearance. CIS victims experience what psychologists call dissociation—spacing out, drifting off, feeling unreal and outside their bodies.

Hey, that sounds like me.

Other CIS markers include panic attacks. Anxiety. Depression. Impatience. Regret. Loneliness. Lack of spontaneity. Chronic embarrassment. A crippling sense of doubt. Recognize those? Most appeared earlier in this book as symptoms of self-loathing.

Prodigious research into ex-cultists reveals even more similarities between them and us. For example, ex-cultists commonly manifest a false self, which psychologists also call a pseudopersonality.

Ex-cultists feel angry at having been used and ashamed at having been deceived.

Ex-cultists have trust issues, family issues, dependency issues, and commitment issues.

Ex-cultists sometimes find it hard to remember their precult lives.

Ex-cultists agonize over basic questions such as what to eat or what to wear.

Ex-cultists constantly ask others for permission, even to do simple activities such as sitting down or closing doors.

Ex-cultists feel irreparably alienated from nearly everyone.

And ex-cultists find it nearly impossible to say no. According to leading cult expert Margaret Thaler Singer, ex-cultists "accept almost everything they hear, as if their pre-cult skills for evaluating and criticizing were in relative abeyance. They cannot listen and judge: they listen, believe, and obey. Simple remarks of friends, dates, coworkers, and roommates are taken as commands" by the ex-cultist, even when he or she "does not feel like doing the bidding, or even abhors it." In other words, ex-cultists cannot say no.

As one ex-cultist told Singer: "Freedom is great. But it takes a lot of work."

Ex-cultists' obedience springs from the fact that cult leaders "prescribed virtually every activity—what and when to eat, wear, and do during the day and night, showering, defecating procedures, and sleep positions. The loss of a way of life in which everything is planned" leaves ex-cultists facing a fearsome "future void" in which "they must plan and execute all their tomorrows on their own," Singer wrote.

Freed prisoners and people struggling to stop hating themselves also face a "future void." *Uh-oh. What next?*

Yes, it's embarrassing for us who hate ourselves to call ourselves ex-cultists. Then again, nearly everything embarrasses us. (Then again, nearly everything embarrasses ex-cultists.) We don't want to wallow in victimhood, call attention to ourselves, or claim to be newsworthy in any way. Nor do we want to minimize the damage done by "real" cults.

But how do ex-cultists heal? If ex-cultists can "deprogram" themselves, can we do so too? To help ex-cultists deprogram themselves, exit counselors use a variety of exercises. For example, ex-cultists are asked to write detailed timelines of their entire cult histories. Revisiting these events via the safe, controllable context of list making helps the ex-cultists process feelings that were suppressed when the events were occurring.

In another exercise, ex-cultists are asked to silently visualize some of their cult experiences with a detached perspective as if watching them on TV. Keeping this distance from the memories helps ex-cultists better understand what has happened to them, and keeps them from re-blaming and re-victimizing themselves.

To defuse their overreaction to environmental triggers (a classic post-trauma symptom) ex-cultists are asked to educate themselves on the dynamics of hypnosis and mind control, to remain conscious of their triggers—because triggers work at the *unconscious* level—and to "re-wire" their triggers to positive, nonthreatening "anchors." For example, ex-members of religious cults who are triggered by the smell of incense or the word *amen* might reduce their reactions to these things by burning incense while watching funny movies and by repeating the word *amen* over and over quickly and continuously until it sounds like meaningless syllables.

Can we adjust these exercises to quell our self-loathing? My worst trigger is hearing people yell. That sound makes me panic even if they're not yelling *at* me, even if they're just yelling to be heard over the roar of a passing train. I associate raised voices with anger, punishment, and emotions spinning out of control. How to recontextualize that? Should I watch a lot of *Three Stooges* episodes? Or attend operas?

What if you were the *only* member of your "cult"? What if

you were the only follower of a leader whose supremacy was unknown to everyone but you? What if you said: *I have escaped! I'm finally free!* and everyone wondered what the heck you meant?

What if they refused to believe that you'd been in a cult because your false self passed for real for so long, so persuasively, that it no longer looked even remotely fake?

It was, it is, this way for me. The version of me that most people see, the version that has walked this world since kindergarten or before, was formed under duress. Since the dawning of consciousness, starting before I can remember, I devoted every thought and act to pleasing someone I feared and adored, someone I aimed to imitate and replicate, someone I yearned to be. She was the most frightened and pessimistic person in the world, but I did not know that then. Looking up from my crib, I thought she was the sky, the universe, a deity. Henceforth I walked this world a hybrid, mostly Mom and marginally me, a clashing patchwork rag doll refracted through friends, boyfriends, and characters in books. Feeble but blustering, dreamy but hopeless, and always the awful hair.

Which is to say, a self almost incapable of independent thought. A hash of rags thinly cloaking successive layers of self-loathing, with a small salvageable sliver stuffed inside. So many times I wanted to say:

I'm not who you think I am.

And:

I'm not who I think I am.

One day when I was twenty-nine, I told my father that I

had furnished my one-bedroom apartment for less than fifty dollars.

You did this smart thing, my father said, *because your mother and I taught you well.*

Taken aback, I countered: *What? It had nothing to do with you. I did the shopping, hauling, building, fixing, painting, planning.*

Dad smiled, shook his head, and gazed upward.

You are the instrument, he said, *by which we work our will.*

Although I was appalled at this statement, the more I thought about it, the more I realized he was correct. While saving money is a virtue, I first learned to save money—as I learned to do everything—in hopes of winning their approval. *Isn't she the smartest little saver in the world?*

Time lost.

I cannot get it back.

Some say freedom is easy but whoever says this is already free.

Stop Being Prejudiced Against Yourself

What is self-loathing but the coldest prejudice of all, a prejudice against the self?

Much self-esteem is lost not when individual spellcasters attack individual victims based on individual characteristics, but when individuals belong to minority groups that are collectively hated or shunned by the majority. Race-, gender-,

sexuality-, ethnicity-, wealth-, ability-, and size-based norma-
tivity has wrought immeasurable damage.

. . .

In Toni Morrison's novel *The Bluest Eye*, each member of an
African-American family experiences self-loathing in a different way. Cholly Breedlove, traumatized by an early sexual experience, rapes his young daughter Pecola. Self-abasing Pecola
wants blue eyes, believing that no one would dare do "bad
things in front of those pretty eyes." Mother Pauline Breedlove
seems to care more for her white employer's child than for
her own.

Spellbound by racial prejudice, the Breedloves hate themselves "as if the master had said, 'You are ugly people.' They
had looked about themselves and saw nothing to contradict the
statement; saw, in fact, support for it leaning at them from every
billboard, every movie, every glance."

In a YouTube video that he posted on May 4, 2011, fourteen-
year-old Jamey Rodemeyer of Buffalo, New York, explained
that after coming out as bisexual to his classmates the previous
fall, "I always got made fun of. . . . They'd be like, 'Faggot!
Fag!' and they'd taunt me in the hallways, and I felt like I could
never escape it." Online, "people would just constantly send me
hate, telling me that gay people go to hell."

In the video, Jamey urged bullied teens to be brave:

"All you have to do is hold your head up and you'll go far. . . .
That's all you have to do. Just love yourself and you're set. I
promise."

"Look at me," Jamey said with a smile. "I'm doing fine."

He wasn't. Four months later, he hanged himself. Some of the messages he had received online were later reprinted in the media.

"JAMIE [sic] IS STUPID, GAY, FAT ANND [sic] UGLY. HE MUST DIE!" one post reportedly read. "I wouldn't care if you died," another reportedly read. "No one would. So just do it :) It would make everyone WAY more happier!"

An individual might feel okay about him- or herself personally, might not hate any aspect of his or her body, characters, or personality—but might ultimately be brought down by prejudice, an automatic weapon that is programmed to target anything displaying the wrong shape, color, size, or lifestyle.

Prejudice is as old as humanity. But humanity is evolving: Published in 1970, *The Bluest Eye* was set in post-Depression America. In many new studies, African-Americans are shown to have higher self-esteem than their white and Hispanic counterparts.

Maybe society *is* changing after all. Yes, people of all shapes, sizes, classes, orientations, and backgrounds still experience low self-esteem. But prejudice is now roundly reviled. Pride movements now thrive that would have been unimaginable fifty years ago.

People with low self-esteem exhibit no outward characteristics that might make us the targets of prejudice from a cruel society. But even so, we *do* suffer from a terrible prejudice; that is, prejudice *by* each of us *against* each of us. Surely this is what the pre-Raphaelite poet Christina Rossetti had in mind when in 1876 she wrote:

I lock my door upon myself,
And bar them out; but who shall wall
Self from myself, most loathed of all?

Just as a bigot irrationally loathes every attribute of a certain demographic, we irrationally loathe every aspect of ourselves. Like bigots ranting *There goes the neighborhood*, we never give ourselves a chance, predicting—incorrectly—our own misbehavior. Just as bigots jeer at caricatures of their hated groups, we imagine—and draw—our bodies as grotesque, just as Mom did when she signed her letters to me with an armed-and-legged circle she called "Fatmom." But because we both feel *and* inflict our shame, no pride movement offers itself for us to join.

What would you tell a bigot if you could stand to spend five minutes with one? *Open your mind. Be tolerant. Everyone has something to offer.*

Even me.

Realize That You Are a Master Craftsman

Imagine a master craftsman or craftswoman. This person is immensely skilled at weaving, say, or carpentry. He or she has augmented inborn talent with arduous training and long practice. Give the weaver any fiber, any loom—anything, really, that can make a warp and weft—and he or she will shine. Equip the carpenter with wood, nails, hammers, blades—and he or she will soar. Ask each to make something: you will receive a perfect rug, the quintessential chair.

But make them switch tasks—give the weaver hammers and wood, the carpenter wool and a loom—and ask them to produce. What would you get?

The results would shock you and shame their makers, because while both the weaver and the carpenter possess exquisite talents, expertise, and gifts, they do not possess the *same* talents, expertise, and gifts.

Each of us has a unique skill set. No matter how much we hate ourselves, we have to admit that we are better at some things than others, maybe even moderately gifted at a few. According to some psychologists, the road to happiness—and out of self-loathing—starts when we recognize those skills and practice using them as much as possible—becoming "master craftspeople," crafting our lives.

"Give up the notion that life is about correcting your weaknesses," says University of Pennsylvania psychology professor Martin Seligman, who spearheaded the new field of "positive psychology."

"I have lots of weaknesses. So do you," asserts Seligman, who spent thirty years studying suicidal depression before switching his focus to happiness. Formerly unhappy people including himself became happy after "we recognized in ourselves that we had certain strengths, we named them and we learned to run with them, to use them to buffer ourselves against the vicissitudes that come our way."

These "signature strengths," as Seligman calls them, are mainly aspects of character. Kindness. Humor. Diligence. Honesty. Creativity. Leadership. Courage. Playfulness. Scholarship. Fairness. The capacity for love.

You might deny having signature strengths. Having low self-esteem, of course you might. You don't want to sound narcissistic, or to lie. But somewhere deep down, confess: *You have strengths.*

You have skills. You have tools. Maybe not the same ones as the person sitting nearest you right now, but like a master craftsman, you have a network of talents, training, and wisdom on which to draw. These strengths inspire you. Motivate you. Make you forget, at least briefly, that you hate yourself.

Studies consistently show that religious people are the happiest people in any given population. Seligman says religious people are happy not because they are literally "saved" or "blessed," but because in their religiosity they have almost certainly identified, prioritized, and activated at least one of their signature strengths: spirituality.

"If we make choices in life that are about aligning ourselves with an increase in knowledge, an increase in power, an increase in goodness"—whatever "increase" our particular strengths compel—"we are on the same path as religious people," Seligman says; that is, the happiest path.

If anything gives our lives meaning, it is recognizing, honing, and *using* our signature strengths. Seligman suggests that each of us identify three or four of these strengths, then reshape our daily routines so as to connect with each of these strengths every single day. So, for example, even with low self-esteem you can admit that you are playful, kind, and have a sense of humor; listen to comedy CDs en route to work; spend time with pets or children; and help others—overtired spouses, sick friends, and tourists lost on street corners.

We who hate ourselves have spent years bashing ourselves for lacking all the strengths we lack while underestimating the strengths we have. Does the weaver lament not being able to discern walnut from cherrywood, or knowing how to plane? For having no idea what a bobbin is, does the carpenter call himself a fool?

Break the Spell

And now it comes to us at last: the strength to break the spell.

Ever since our prehistoric ancestors performed the first of what we might call rites—dancing, sacrifice, those Paleolithic burial rituals conducted three hundred thousand years ago in Iraq's Shanidar Cave, which might have entailed hollyhocks—as long as our species has known spirituality, it has known magic: good and bad. Our ancestors kept busy, breaking spells.

With what?

Purification: water, fire. Create a symbol of your spellcaster, your story, your false self, and burn it or dissolve it. Burial: Create a symbol, as above. Bury it solemnly or joyously. Consider singing, dancing, or pissing on graves.

Visualization, Version 1: In a place where you will not be disturbed, close your eyes and revisit your spellcasting. Tell yourself you have returned for yourself. Picture, in as much detail as possible, a rescue. Visualization, Version 2: In a place where you will not be disturbed, close your eyes and create a mental symbol representing your self-loathing. Picture, in as much detail as possible, destroying it. Imagine smashing it, dropping it into acid, hacking it to bits.

Prayer: If you believe in deities or higher powers, call on these to consecrate the breaking of the spell. Ask to be witnessed. Ask for grace.

Whichever option you select, as soon as you have finished it, begin another rite to mark your start, from this point on. This is a rite of transformation and rebirth. This could entail immersion. Music. Planting. Art. Climbing to mountaintops. What symbolizes hope to you? What symbolizes life?

Healing Takes Time

Rivers know this; there is no hurry.
We shall get there some day.

—A. A. MILNE

Have patience with everything that
remains unsolved in your heart.

—RAINER MARIA RILKE

Here we are: almost all the way out of self-loathing. Almost all the way to medium. To get this far, you went back into your own past to meet yourself again as you were then. Reaching back to seize your younger hand, you resisted your urge to turn and run. You made yourself watch yourself almost die ten thousand times. You sat back there as your own witness, seeing what was, grasping the truth with which you set yourself free.

Which is, if you think about it, quite an achievement.

Okay, then.

Now what?

Because at this point you might be thinking: *If I've discovered so much, if I'm now so smart, why do I still hurt like hell?*

This is the question of the century. We who have hated ourselves ask it every day.

Work hard at anything—completing tax forms, mining copper, cleaning house—and you might justifiably believe that you deserve a prize, a celebration, a reward. Work hard at understanding why we hated ourselves and what happens?

Well, in a best-case scenario, we stop hating ourselves. Done. You can close this book and have some fun.

But, better than anyone else, we know: *Best-case scenario? Don't make me laugh.* Because things rarely go as planned.

This is the point at which we have to choose. Hating ourselves was not at first a choice. It was forced on us. But beyond the Land of Now You Know, self-loathing is a choice. Now that we know all we know, we heal if we choose to heal.

Healing takes time.

The act of escaping from self-loathing is not a sudden stroke of good fortune like winning the lottery or having a life-saving operation. One is not transformed, fixed, all set forever overnight. Escaping from self-loathing is a slow and steady journey on a bumpy, vaguely uphill grade. You go a ways. You stop. You go a ways, remaining ever sensitive (although less than before) to certain triggers—gestures, places, words—but treating yourself like a buddy who has certain sensitivities. You go a ways. You learn. You go a ways. You stop, fall, and freak out. You get up. Go a ways. *You go.*

It takes time because, enchanted, we had a problem but did not know what it was. Had you asked me ten years ago *What is your problem?* I would have said: *My problem is that I am ugly and incompetent and gross.*

Leaving the prison of self-loathing feels at first like losing our minds because we see in such sharp relief what we put up with for so long.

Awareness cannot cure us instantly because habits are hard to break. We hated ourselves for so long that, were we not extremely careful henceforth, we run the risk of hating ourselves reflexively. We do not want or plan to hate ourselves. Who would? We say *Tsk-tsk, not gonna hate myself this time.* But then. And then. At least at first, we have to watch our every move.

It takes time because we have been harming ourselves so fervently and in so many places for so long. Some of us have spent our whole lives committing suicide.

And some of us survived.

. . .

But oh, the wait.

Spellcasters put us here. Consigned us to this darkness, whether they meant to or not. And we stayed here mainly by our own unwitting will. We slumped in resignation, as if drugged, or shook with misdirected rage. But mainly we mistook waiting for life.

Could we still call it patience when we did not know that we were even waiting, much less what we were waiting for? When in fact we were really biding time, scolding ourselves? Such darkness is narcotic, numbing us to our wounds and the ticking of the clock.

After she was raped by a fan at age twenty-one, the singer Tori Amos spent many years struggling to regain her sexual trust and sense of self.

"To heal the wound, you have to go into the dark night of the soul. . . . It's taken me a long time to be a woman," Amos said fifteen years after the rape. "I have a really good shrink, and we started 'beading a necklace,' as she calls it. This much at a time: a little bead here, a little bead there—a memory, a moment, and then one day something shifted. You can get there. You can get there."

Waiting, waiting, forever waiting: it *would* be forever too had we said nothing, done nothing, to save ourselves. Had we not shrieked at each other and at ourselves: *Wake up.* Wake up and call yourself by name, as do those who know they exist.

Waiting, waiting, forever waiting, but for what? We dared not wonder, dared not know, for knowing would reveal the magnitude of what has never been and what might never be, or worse: what *has* been which we missed. By miraculous intervention and true grit we crawled out of the dark, and then into the light only to see how late it was. We felt exactly as one might after sitting through an entire fireworks show with eyes closed, opening them only at the final moment as the last sparkles dissolve. We thought: *Too late.* We thought: *I should have kept my eyes shut, because it hurts to know what I missed.*

Would it be better never to have known?

One never wishes one could wear cashmere if one has never heard of it. One never regrets never having swum the turquoise waters off Oahu if one has never heard of Oahu. Are those who never heard of Oahu better off or worse than those who know the name *Oahu* yet have never been? Which ones are cursed, which blessed? Because now that we are out of the darkness, we must face the fact that we might know too much.

And can you handle that? This knowledge blinding as the sun?

You can. It's not too late. Remember the expression *He who laughs last, laughs longest*? That's us—the ones who laugh last. In which case, we win. Those who never hated themselves have laughed and laughed. Lucky them. We who laugh last are just learning how. But with the incandescent wonder that surrounds the new. *It's our turn.*

Laugh.

* * *

Identify your saints.

You have known spellcasters. You have known spellcasters' assistants. You have known the ones who harmed you on purpose or accidentally, the ones who watched and did nothing at all.

But all along that path, you have had heroes. Saviors. Saints. They were the ones who saw and understood, the ones who looked you in the eye. The ones who tried.

Your saints might not have been the most *prominent* people in your life—the most physically present, longest-term, or closest kin. Some of them drifted through, some hovered briefly. Some you never even knew.

After one of the most humiliating events of my life—wetting myself in a middle-school history class because self-loathing made me too afraid to ask for permission to go to the restroom—my teacher, quietly appalled, sent me to the school nurse.

This nurse's name was Mrs. Holcomb. On that Day of Great Humiliation, she was about forty, with short, curly brick-red hair.

Giving me soap and washcloths and a clean new pair of gym shorts from a stack of such things she kept in a drawer, she let me sob.

Have a good cry, she said. And then:

I'm a square-dancer, Mrs. Holcomb said. *My husband, Ace, and I, we square-dance every Sunday at the club. We sure have fun! Okay, one Sunday we were dancing when somebody made a joke. I don't remember what it was about—some little thing. One of the ladies—my friend Janice—laughed. She got the giggles and she laughed so hard! Yes, guess what happened. Just like you! She couldn't help it, right there in her pretty square-dance outfit in the middle of the floor. She was embarrassed! Yes! But you know what? We said: Don't worry, honey, this could have happened to anyone.*

Because it could! Mrs. Holcomb handed me a Kleenex. *See?*

Which was exactly the right thing to say to me right then. So Mrs. Holcomb, dead or alive, is a saint.

My friend Ruby finds her saints in films.

"During an especially bad period of my life a few years ago, I watched a lot of war movies, because the best ones glorify the incredible endurance people have shown in wars, knowing that they cannot win personally, or that they might not live to see victory, but that they must do their humble part," Ruby told me. "Besides which, they tend to put one's own problems into perspective! *The Great Escape* is a good example of this, or *The Dirty Dozen.*

"One of my favorites is the Cold War series *The Sandbaggers.* The protagonist has failed at many things and knows it; he is all too aware of his own flaws. He had a disastrous marriage, and once he bungled a mission because he was drunk and got someone killed—because of this he never touches alcohol. But he knows that his work in the British Secret Service is important, much more important than his own life or his own ego, and so he keeps on getting out of bed every morning and giving his all. This is something that often gets me through: remembering that I can still achieve something of use to the world even if I personally am not what I would have wanted to be."

Who were your saints and why? How can you honor them today?

. . .

And now, recovery: Chronic sorrow is a strange thing from which to have to free oneself because it is such a silly thing to have. That's it, a *silly* thing. Almost a *sin.* Why on earth would most of us suffer chronic sorrow, in this country, in this age of high science and luxury? Why you? Why me? Because we were put under spells.

How do snakes feel while shedding their skins? How do caterpillars feel while turning into butterflies? We cannot ask. They cannot tell.

The trouble with being in a cocoon is that, for a while at

least, you are transitional. The only thing you know for sure is that you are no longer a caterpillar. Not yet a butterfly, but close; it's going to happen, whether you plan for it or not. You are changing from within. Old parts in there are withering and vanishing—like extra legs.

Soon you will dry your fresh wings in the sun. And then take flight.

. . .

And we feel naked, stupid, scared.

Forging our post–self-loathing selves feels like starting from scratch. It isn't, because our real selves whom we were born to be are in there somewhere.

And some of us can only conjure up worst-case scenarios.

Long ago, in my "time before," when I was still my true self, daydreams danced in my head. Buried under every four-leaf clover was a castle. In beach breezes I heard sea-gods wielding whelk shells, blasting warnings. I thought pigs the size of pinkies walked around tiny Londons and Tokyos under our beds as we slept, and left us notes inscribed on scrolls that most mistook for dust. I thought of fruit-punch fountains, magic horseshoes, phantom ships. I thought birds talked to me, their black eyes desperately urging me to understand.

I lived in dreams, but tell your dreams too often to the wrong people—*because they bade you tell them*—and they will be used against you. *Did you fail that math test,* Mom asked, *because you were thinking about punch fountains?* You come to understand that fantasies are one more thing for which you can and will be punished, one more thing by which you can be judged.

You come to understand that fantasies are flights away from *them*, your spellcasters, and thus fantasies are abandonments. You feel guilty for this. You come to understand that dreams can save you only for a while, but then you must return to the real world. To them. And then.

You come to understand that your spellcasters can read your mind, or at least they say they can, the same way God hears prayers. If they can read your mind, then they can see your dreams. You do not want this. You stop dreaming.

Your spellcasters demand, *Tell the truth!* You come to understand that fantasies are not the truth. In which case they are lies. And lies are crimes. Mom said liars are worse than thieves. Thus fantasies are burglaries.

"Life is a dream," Virginia Woolf wrote. "'Tis waking that kills us. He who robs us of our dreams robs us of our life."

We cannot fantasize because we think we have no right to secrecy or privacy, that were our dreams revealed the world would say: *How silly. How seditious. How perverse.*

Some of us have forgotten how to picture happiness. We have beaten it out of ourselves. We think the only safe dreams are dreams about what could possibly go wrong because these are not fantasies per se. They are penalties. Plans.

Like cult members, we have been told to fear the outside world. We do. Dreams are the world outside the outside world. We fear ourselves in the unknown. We fear the unknown in ourselves.

But see, your dreams have been there waiting for you all along. Those tiny pigs are still under the bed. Those fruit-punch fountains flow. You left them, but they lived, hoping for *you.* They knew.

• • •

The last time I talked with my mother before the delirium began that stayed with her for three weeks until she died, she told me: *I feel like a sack of shit. Because that's what I am.*

Many of her worst fears had come true. She had been correct all along!

When she became delirious, I took her to the hospital. By then, she had no idea who I was and never would again. I sat beside her bed, watching hospital staff whisk in and out, arranging tubes.

At first, her slack face was a mask, vouchsafing not a single clue.

And then she started speaking. Urgently, albeit still delirious, she said:

Can I go now? Where is the boss?

I started typing everything she said. For three days, I did this.

Hello, take your scissors, she said, staring straight ahead. She never looked my way. *Patrick!* she said as if to someone standing there. *You never know when you will need your scissors.*

We received a package just now. It contained crystal and rubber. Hello! I said hello! Has he moved to Palm Springs? How are you today, sir? Joe? You have a midget dog? Oh help yourself.

Her hands moved, pantomiming slicing cake.

What's your idea of fun? she asked, still staring straight ahead, looking intensely curious. *Oh, Max is waving to me! Anyone else wanna give me a hug or a shake?*

And I thought: *Who the hell is this? Why did I never know this cheery, breezy, party-going soul? This smiling, carefree, pleasant total stranger?*

This was she as she would otherwise have been. If she had never been enchanted. This was herself not hating herself.

Joy, can you cut a piece for me? Oh really? Herbie—this is a sort of parade. Help me get on the ship. A Spanish-speaking lady needs to breathe.

*   *   *

How many years did you waste on self-loathing? How many more will you waste? Say it together: *Not one minute more.*

What have we sacrificed for our self-loathing? What did we give away? What did we give up? What did we miss that others experienced under similar circumstances save one difference between us and them? A difference neither of appearance, aptitude, nor heritage, nor anything that could be measured with a microscope or MRI machine. The difference between us and everyone who has never hated themselves cannot be measured scientifically. Were we to all stand side by side, we would look much alike. Shoulders somewhat more slopey on the post-self-loathers, maybe? Shyer smiles?

Deep down, in our vestigial hopeful places, most of us have always known that we were not so horrible. We just could not accept, admit, apply, or even bear to think these words. We knew them with a kind of certainty that hummed almost inaudibly, then sometimes bloomed, then burned up swiftly like old film in a projector, *flap flap flap.*

We could not fight to save ourselves, because the rule was that we could not fight, that we would always lose. Whatever happened, they would pound us to the ground.

Now when you wake, rules break. First with a whoosh came the words *I am not so horrible,* and you believe it now. And oh:

I have suffered for nothing.

This concept could set us free. Suffered? For *nothing*? Well, jeez, stop—just as, the instant you realize a rock is in your shoe, you shake it out. Ouch! Not one millisecond more!

But say you had walked with that rock inside your shoe for five blocks. Say you had walked that way for five miles. Say you had walked that way for *fifty miles* and never shook it out. Because you did not know it was a rock, you believed it was part of you. Because you did not know you could. Good riddance, while still good, is weighted with regret. Because we are at last awake and the first rule of wakefulness is *stop hating yourself,* we must with all our might battle the impulse to blame ourselves for walking all those miles with that rock. Because self-blame, in the final analysis, is the very thing we're trying to shake out.

You know how good it feels to remove a rock from your shoe? Remember doing that? Sheer bliss, better than walking in those same shoes had they *never* held a rock. Because—that rock taught you what hurting was. No rock, you never would have known.

Lesson complete. *Shake, shake.*

. . .

I am not absolutely cured.

I am significantly better. I no longer *hate* myself. I would no longer run around the house jabbing my stomach with a knife. I can say no. I am at medium sometimes. Most of the time.

I cannot pretend to be absolutely cured.

I cannot lie and say: *Do exactly what I did and you will be cured.*

I cannot lie because lies literally made me sick. The more I lie, the sicker I will stay.

I must be honest with you—and myself. This too is part of the new post–self-loathing me: truth. Telling the truth about my weaknesses makes me less weak. Funny how that works. An anti-vicious cycle. An elysian wheel.

I cannot lie and tell you I am *absolutely* cured but I can say: *I'm better.*

This is big. That I can walk and talk without fearing what others will say: this is epiphanic. Otherworldly. *This* is big.

We who hate ourselves are like people born with perfect vision who were prescribed horror-colored glasses long ago, and squinted at the world through them for years. Remove those glasses. *You can see.*

How did my own mother do this to me? How could she?

How did she become this way herself? She was teased as a child for being overweight. Was this enough to wreck her life, then ripple through and ruin mine? I suspect not. I suspect something else happened to her back then, something much worse, but we will never know. She never spoke of it. She was brave to have hated herself so much yet stayed here so long.

Sometimes, these days, soft sea foam sweeps the sparkling sand and swathes my feet as I stand *not* regretting things. Instead, I can just stand there smelling salted air. That this happens even at least sometimes is huge.

Who is this medium-size figure standing on the sand, whose grains the afternoon sunshine turns copper, emerald, electrum, gold? Whoever she is, she is not as she once was. She is not always thinking awful things about herself. She is not always thinking awful things. She is not always thinking of herself. What joy, that there is such a possibility as joy.

I wear prescription glasses, take allergy pills, and obscure certain scars with cream. No product I can buy would fix my self-esteem. There is no simple fix. Exhorting me to have high self-esteem, *just have it,* is like telling me to just read magazines without my glasses. Some would tell me to smile into mirrors, as my friend Kelly used to do, saying *Hello, beautiful. Hello, beautiful.* That approach is overkill. I would die laughing first.

To flourish as ourselves, to simply be ourselves, we must conquer the selves that war against ourselves. We have no choice.

We have no choice in this world but—in this and this alone—to give ourselves no choice.

Stop thinking of yourself. This will feel weird at first, then like relief.

Interrupt the self-loathing voice, then in those split seconds of peace remind yourself that in the world at large, nothing has much to do with you.

Ironically, this works.

Realize your insignificance to the stars and the cosmos, your tininess compared to the magnitude of just one sea.

Then look around and ask yourself: *Is this in any way—in any any any way—a nice day?* Sure it is. Do you have money in your pocket? Do you not have leprosy? Are your children alive? Is your town not under invasion? Can you see trees? Can you see?

Aha!

This is more work than most folks do all week. Yet we who are in recovery from low self-esteem must do it many times each day. This is what separates us from the world. This work. What others receive automatically—the optimism, confidence, and self-acceptance that they take for granted—we wrest from the world only through daily knock-down, drag-out fights. Upside: this makes us treasure our hard-won joys more. We take no laugh for granted. For us, *Have a nice day* is a battle cry.

I raise that battle cry and tell myself it makes me strong. The yellow smiley faces on the blanket on my bed are kitsch but also not. I tell myself that every split second in which I save myself again is an epiphany.

I am not absolutely cured, but I have this. Five dollars in my pocket, and no leprosy.

How did I get here? Not by chanting *Hello, beautiful.*

I got here nice day by nice day, cool breeze by cool breeze. Tiny victory by tiny victory. My education is my scrutiny of normal people doing normal things. Their normalcy in its simplicity is holy. I watch a girl on a bus brushing her hair, cocking her head at her reflection in the window glass with neither love nor hate. I think: *I want to be like her.* I watch a chef cooking food at a restaurant and I can tell he is not thinking about himself. He is too busy, too interested in his work. I think: *I want to be like him.* Sometimes, I am.

And glad.

BENEDICTION: SELF TO SELF

Always with you,

All forgiven,

All days new days,

Safe with me.

Notes

INTRODUCTION

3   "I've always had really low self-esteem": Caris Davis and Stephen M. Silverman, "Mariah Carey: I've Always Had Low Self-Esteem," *People*, March 18, 2008.

19   Studies reveal skyrocketing self-esteem: Roy F. Baumeister, et al., "Does High Self-Esteem Cause Better Performance, Interpersonal Success, Happiness, or Healthier Lifestyles?" *Psychological Science in the Public Interest*, May 2003.

19   In fact, many recent studies: Nicholas Emler, et al., "The Costs and Causes of Low Self-Worth," commissioned by the Joseph Rowntree Foundation, November 2001.

CHAPTER 1

39   In one study, whose purpose: Philippe Rochat and Tricia Striano, "Emerging Self-Exploration by 2-Month-Old Infants," *Developmental Science*, 2:2, 1999.

40   In one study, eighteen-month-old: David M. Sobel and Natasha Z. Kirkham, "Blickets and Babies: The Development of Causal Reasoning in Toddlers and Infants," *Developmental Psychology*, 2006, vol. 42, no. 6.

40   In one study, researchers played games: William J. Cromie, "Long-Term Memory Kicks in After Age One," *Harvard Gazette*, November 7, 2002.

44   "The infant and young child should experience": Inge Bretherton, "The Origins of Attachment Theory: John Bowlby and Mary Ainsworth," *Developmental Psychology*, September 1992.

44 "When those *primal needs* are not met": J. Konrad Stettbacher, *Making Sense of Suffering: The Healing Confrontation with Your Own Past* (New York: E. P. Dutton, 1991).

46 In one study, researchers set out: Stuart Wolpert, "UCLA Psychologists Discover a Gene's Link to Optimism, Self-Esteem," UCLA Newsroom, September 13, 2011.

47 These variances "are not just differences": Steven Pinker, "Human Nature and the Blank Slate," TED Talks, February 6, 2003.

49 According to one biographer, Franz Kafka's: Reiner Stach, *Franz Kafka: The Decisive Years* (New York: Houghton Mifflin, 2005).

54 "Some of us are born with a sense of loss": Gloria Vanderbilt, *A Mother's Story* (New York: Plume, 1997).

55 Before she was a world-famous actress: Eloise Parker, "Kate Winslet: Kids Used to Call Me 'Blubber' in School," *New York Daily News*, April 29, 2009.

57 "Just as soon as children develop awareness": Alice Miller, *For Your Own Good: Hidden Cruelty in Child-Rearing and the Roots of Violence* (New York: Farrar, Straus & Giroux, 1990).

57 Biracial actress Halle Berry: Joyce Maynard, "Roles of a Lifetime: Halle Berry," *New York Times Magazine,* October 18, 2012.

58 "I remember just clinging to the metal": Shannon Lambert, appearing on *20/20,* February 15, 1999.

60 Deeming desire and hatred: Geshe Lhundup Sopa and Jeffrey Hopkins, *Cutting Through Appearances: Practice and Theory of Tibetan Buddhism* (Boston, MA: Snow Lion, 1989).

60 The spiritual teacher Eckhart Tolle: Eckhart Tolle, "Are Thoughts the Source of Ego?" Eckhart Tolle TV, May 2010.

64 Buddhist teacher Pema Chödrön tells us: "How We Get Hooked and How We Get Unhooked," *Shambhala Sun,* March 2003.

66 "The brain is very 'sticky'": Rick Hanson, interview with the author.

67 In one such study, magnetic resonance: W. R. Marchand, "Mindfulness-Based Stress Reduction, Mindfulness-Based Cognitive Therapy, and Zen Meditation for Depression, Anxiety, Pain, and Psychological Distress," *Journal of Psychiatric Practice,* July 2012.

75 "Soul murder is neither a diagnosis nor a condition": Leonard Shengold, *Soul Murder: The Effects of Childhood Abuse and Deprivation* (New York: Ballantine Books, 1991).

75 "You trade your reality for a role": Lizze James, "Jim Morrison: Ten Years Gone," *Creem,* Summer 1981.

75 In Henrik Ibsen's 1879 play *A Doll's House*: Henrik Ibsen, *A Doll's House* (Mineola, NY: Dover Editions, 1992).

Notes

76 Ibsen revisited soul murder: Henrik Ibsen, *Four Major Plays* (New York: Signet Classics, 1995).

81 "Sometimes I don't feel as if I'm a person": Dorian Lynskey, "David Bowie: The Godfather of Ch-ch-change," *The Observer*, September 8, 2012.

CHAPTER 2

94 As the businessman Hank Rearden philosophizes: Ayn Rand, *Atlas Shrugged* (New York: Plume, 1999).

98 Unsurprisingly, studies show: Haojuan Tao, et al., "Depression Uncouples Brain Hate Circuit," *Molecular Psychology*, October 2011.

101 Oliver Wendell Homes called apology: Holmes, Oliver Wendell. *The Writings of Oliver Wendell Holmes*, Volume 2 (New York: Houghton Mifflin, 1892).

104 "There were two Venus Williamses": Oprah Winfrey, "Oprah Talks to Venus and Serena Williams," *O, the Oprah Magazine*, March 2003.

110 "It was only necessary to be happy": Franz Kafka, *Dearest Father* (London: Oneworld Classics, 2009).

119 "The world may observe academic success": D. W. Winnicott, *The Maturational Process and the Facilitating Environment: Studies in the Theory of Emotional Development* (London: Hogarth Press, 1965).

122 "Live quietly in the moment": Paramahansa Yogananda, *Autobiography of a Yogi* (Los Angeles, CA: Self-Realization Fellowship, 1998).

123 "What you think of as the past": Eckhart Tolle, *The Power of Now* (Novato, CA: New World Library, 1999).

126 And really, what praise could penetrate: Elaine Blair, "Great American Losers," *New York Review of Books* blog, http://www.nybooks .com/blogs/nyrblog/2012/mar/09/great-american-losers/. Gary Shteyngart, *Super Sad True Love Story* (New York: Random House, 2010).

128 "The least little blemish drew tears from my eyes": Mohandas Gandhi, *All Men Are Brothers* (London: Continuum, 1980).

131 Mariel Hemingway watched: Nicole Lampert, "Daddy Abused Both My Sisters . . . but He Wasn't a Monster: Ernest Hemingway's Granddaughter Reveals a Shocking Twist in Family's History of Alcoholism and Suicide," *Daily Mail*, February 14, 2013.

131 A 2013 Australian study: Tracey D. Wade and Marika Tiggeman, "The Role of Perfectionism in Body Dissatisfaction," *Journal of Eating Disorders*, January 2013.

132 While a certain amount of perfectionism: [no author] "Perfectionism and Eating Disorders: Complex Issue," *Science Daily*, January 22, 2013.

Notes

132 "As perfectionists go about their day-to-day lives": [no author] "Binge Eating: When Perfection Unravels," *Science Daily*, April 20, 2009.

137 In a letter to his disciplinarian father: Franz Kafka, *Dearest Father* (London: Oneworld Classics, 2009).

137 One study explored: Linda Pfiffner and S. J. O'Leary, "Effects of Maternal Discipline and Nurturance on Toddlers' Behavior and Affect," *Journal of Abnormal Child Psychology*, October 1989.

138 "The conviction that parents are always right": Alice Miller, *For Your Own Good: Hidden Cruelty in Child-Rearing and the Roots of Violence* (New York: Farrar, Straus & Giroux, 1990).

142 "I've gone through stages": Fiona Apple, interview, November 1997, http://www.neverisapromise.com/interviews/Interview97.html.

CHAPTER 3

158 "It calls out, screams": J. Konrad Stettbacher, *Making Sense of Suffering: The Healing Confrontation with Your Own Past* (New York: E. P. Dutton, 1991).

159 Some of our spellcasters might have admired: Alice Miller, *For Your Own Good: Hidden Cruelty in Child-Rearing and the Roots of Violence* (New York: Farrar, Straus & Giroux, 1990).

163 In Virginia Woolf's novel *Mrs. Dalloway*: Virginia Woolf, *Mrs. Dalloway* (New York: Random House, 1993).

171 "Marry, and you will regret it": Søren Kierkegaard, *Either/Or* (Princeton, NJ: Princeton University Press, 1987).

172 Charged with embezzling more than $300,000: Mark Russell, "Secretary Stole Thousands Because She 'Felt Worthless,'" *The Age*, June 15, 2012.

173 Asked about his history of violence: Hal Boedeker, "Mike Tyson Tells Katie Couric, 'I Hated Myself,'" *Orlando Sentinel*, February 7, 2013.

174 After Step 9, the "Big Book": Bill W. and Dr. Bob, *Alcoholics Anonymous: The Story of How Many Thousands of Men and Women Have Recovered from Alcoholism* (New York: Alcoholics Anonymous World Services, 1976).

179 A woman with a rare genetic disorder: Justin S. Feinstein et al., "The Human Amygdala and the Induction and Experience of Fear," *Current Biology*, December 2010.

180 "I was a coward": Mohandas Gandhi, *All Men Are Brothers* (London: Continuum, 1980).

181 Shining the bright light of consciousness: [no author] "That Giant Tarantula Is Terrifying, But I'll Touch It," *Science Daily*, September 4, 2012.

Notes

182 In *The Wonderful Wizard of Oz*, he snaps: L. Frank Baum, *The Wonderful World of Oz* (New York: Signet Classics, 2006).

185 We don't want to be scary: William Wordsworth and Samuel Taylor Coleridge, *Lyrical Ballads* (New York: Penguin Classics, 2007).

188 Although post-traumatic stress disorder is well-known: Judith Herman, *Trauma and Recovery* (New York: Basic Books, 1997).

192 *The Chronicles of Narnia* author C. S. Lewis: C. S. Lewis, *Of Other Worlds* (London: First Harvest, 1975).

194 A letter that the French novelist: Gustave Flaubert, *The Letters of Gustave Flaubert, 1830–1857* (Cambridge, MA: Harvard University Press, 1980).

196 In Sophie Kinsella's novel *Remember Me?*: Sophie Kinsella, *Remember Me?* (New York: Random House, 2008).

198 "The initial symbiotic relationship between mother and child": Alice Miller, *For Your Own Good: Hidden Cruelty in Child-Rearing and the Roots of Violence* (New York: Farrar, Straus & Giroux, 1990).

198 "Every child has an urgent need for good parenting": Leonard Shengold, *Soul Murder Revisited: Thoughts About Therapy, Hate, Love, and Memory* (New Haven, CT: Yale University Press, 2000).

200 When Steven Hassan joined Reverend Sun Myung Moon's Unification Church: Steven Hassan, *Combatting Mind Control* (Rochester, VT: Park Street Press, 1988).

203 In a series of studies, researchers played: Joel Schwartz, "People with Low Self-Esteem Less Motivated to Break a Negative Mood," University of Washington press release, August 5, 2002.

205 "Your doubt can become a good quality if you *train* it": Rainer Maria Rilke, *Letters to a Young Poet* (New York: W. W. Norton, 1993).

206 "O, what a rogue and peasant slave am I!": William Shakespeare, *Hamlet* (New York: Simon & Schuster, 2003).

208 In one study, a group of people with low self-esteem: Joanne Wood, et al., "Positive Self-Statements: Power for Some, Peril for Others," *Psychological Science*, May 21, 2009.

209 Kristin Neff, an associate professor: interview with the author.

CHAPTER 4

212 We don't want to become egomaniacs: Albert Camus, *The Fall* (New York: Vintage, 1991).

213 One long-term study found that college students are now twice as narcissistic: Jean M. Twenge and Joshua Foster, "Birth Cohort Increases in Narcissistic Personality Traits Among American College Students, 1982–2009," *Social Psychological and Personality Science*, January 2010.

Notes

213 And other studies show that the so-called Millennial Generation: Jean M. Twenge, "Millennials: The Greatest Generation or the Most Narcissistic?" *The Atlantic*, May 2012.

214 "Certain forms of high self-esteem seem to increase": Roy F. Baumeister, et al., "Relation of Threatened Egotism to Violence and Aggression: The Dark Side of High Self-Esteem," *Psychological Review*, January 1996.

214 "Something striking has happened": Martin Seligman, *The Optimistic Child: A Proven Program to Safeguard Children Against Depression and Build Lifelong Resilience* (New York: Houghton Mifflin Harcourt, 2007).

215 "One has only to go into a prison": Theodore Dalrymple, "Self-Esteem vs. Self-Respect," *In Character*, March 28, 2010, http://incharacter .org/features/theodore-dalrymple-on-self-esteem-vs-self-respect/.

216 A comprehensive review of self-esteem research: Roy F. Baumeister, et al., "Does High Self-Esteem Cause Better Performance, Interpersonal Success, Happiness, or Healthier Lifestyles?" *Psychological Science in the Public Interest*, May 2003.

217 According to the *Tao Te Ching*: Lao Tzu and Stephen Mitchell, *Tao Te Ching* (New York: Harper Perennial, 1992).

217 "Beware of practicing your righteousness": *Holy Bible: King James Version* (New York: American Bible Society, 1980).

CHAPTER 5

226 "Years pass, and prison simply becomes the place": Michael Powell, "Release from Prison: Shock or Growth?" posted at the website of Thubten Chodron, abbess of Sravasti Abbey, http://www.thubtencho dron.org/PrisonDharma/release_from_prison.html.

229 "When you feel bad": interview with the author.

230 "It's a lot easier to feel compassion": interview with the author.

234 Brent Jeffs was born: *I Escaped a Cult*, National Geographic Channel documentary, first aired April 10, 2012.

234 Pat Conroy based his novel: Pat Conroy, *The Great Santini* (New York: Dial Press, 2002).

238 According to leading cult expert: Margaret Thaler Singer, "Coming Out of the Cults," *Psychology Today*, January 1979.

242 In Toni Morrison's novel: Toni Morrison, *The Bluest Eye* (New York: Vintage, 2007).

243 Some of the messages he had received: Susan Donaldson James, "Gay Buffalo Teen Commits Suicide on Eve of National Bullying Summit," ABC News, September 21, 2011.

Notes

245 "Give up the notion": Martin Seligman, appearing on TVO program "Allan Gregg in Conversation: Martin Seligman Believes You Can Make Yourself Happy," first aired February 7, 2002.

CHAPTER 6

252 "To heal the wound": Tori Amos, appearing on *20/20*, February 15, 1999.
257 "Life is a dream": Virginia Woolf, *Orlando* (New York: Mariner Books, 1973).